Aunt Adelade,

It's not "Tales
From the Redskins Sideline," but
it plays great for our audience
down here. And I know
Uncle Kim would have enjoyed
it.

Love,

Chris

M000033453

Tales from the
BUCS SIDELINE

A COLLECTION OF THE GREATEST
BUCS STORIES EVER TOLD

Chris Harry
Joey Johnston

Foreword by Rich McKay

Sports Publishing L.L.C.
www.SportsPublishingLLC.com

© 2004 Chris Harry and Joey Johnston
All Rights Reserved.

Director of production: Susan M. Moyer
Acquisitions editor: Dean Reinke
Project manager: Kathryn R. Holleman
Developmental editor: Doug Hoepker
Graphic designer: Joseph Brumleve
Imaging: Kerri Baker, Christine Mohrbacher, and
Kenneth J. O'Brien
Copy editor: Cynthia L. McNew
Marketing manager: Mike Hagan

ISBN: 1-58261-773-2

Printed in the United States of America.

Sports Publishing L.L.C.
www.SportsPublishingLLC.com

In memory of Tom Ford, a friend and mentor to both of us.

CONTENTS

FOREWORD

It hit me on the flight home from San Diego on January 27, 2003, the day after Super Bowl XXXVII. One of the pilots made an announcement on the intercom, telling us to look out the right side of the airplane.

That's when I saw the lights and said to myself, "My God, this really is big!"

If you were in the stands that night, or watching on television, I'm sure you'll never forget that feeling of absolute euphoria. The Tampa Bay Buccaneers were on top of the world. The whole community—deservedly so—was along for the ride.

It seemed like Dale Mabry Highway was completely blocked. Raymond James Stadium was full. I knew people were happy, but I didn't expect something like this.

I'm not sure who had the original idea to call them the Tampa Bay Buccaneers, but it was a brilliant move. You won't find Tampa Bay on a map. It's just a body of water, not an actual town. That term alone—Tampa Bay—is symbolic of what the franchise meant to the entire area. To people in Tampa, it was their team. St. Petersburg, same thing. Clearwater, Lakeland, Bradenton, Sarasota, Pasco County, Hernando County, right on up and down the line. The franchise became a unifying force.

I must admit, when my father left the University of Southern California to become coach of the expansion Tampa Bay Bucs prior to the 1976 season, I had no idea where Tampa was located in the state of Florida. My mother and I pulled out the encyclopedia and we must have searched for 10 minutes before finding it. We were looking near Miami.

My original plan was to stay in California and finish my senior year in high school. But Hugh Culverhouse, the Bucs' owner, convinced me to join my family because it was going to be a difficult year for my father. Boy, was Mr. C right! As everybody knows, the Bucs didn't win at all that first season and kept losing until the streak reached 26 games. At times, it was unbearable.

But my father wasn't so much concerned about winning a game as he was building something that would last. His perseverance paid off when the Bucs reached the playoffs three times and almost made it to the Super Bowl in 1979.

Then came the drought, the 14 consecutive losing seasons, when the franchise became the butt of jokes everywhere. Even though I wasn't associated with the team for many of those years, it wasn't a pleasant feeling. You'd be visiting out of town somewhere and you'd say that you lived in Tampa and it would generate a remark like, "My gosh, that football team … just awful!" That just didn't seem right. You want your sports teams to do well because it becomes the way your community is identified throughout the country.

When I joined the front office in 1992 and was promoted to general manager two years later, I was naïve enough to think that I could have an impact. I definitely knew that the Tampa Bay area should be having a better experience with its NFL team. Many of the fans not only didn't like the Bucs, they were completely embarrassed by the team. That had to change.

So did the attitude throughout our organization. When we were trying to figure out where the franchise had gone off track, I kept hearing, "If we could just get to 8-8." I almost started to believe that. But you have to be about winning a championship. If you're trying for mediocrity, you won't even get that far. Slowly, our mindset changed.

I never believed in "Buc Luck." I didn't think the franchise was cursed or jinxed. Bad teams lose. Good teams win. It's that simple. The franchise made its own luck. The Bucs drafted Bo Jackson, didn't sign him and lost him. The Bucs traded Steve Young. I never saw that as bad luck. It was just bad—period.

If the Bucs had won just one or two games at the beginning, the franchise's lasting perception would have been different. Even years later, the whole 0-26 thing continued to be a cloud over the franchise. Then it just became a bad franchise and it did the things that bad franchises do. It got rid of good players. It lost close games. And it had nothing to do with luck.

The whole thing reminded me of Bill Murray in *Groundhog Day*. The seasons all ran together, and nothing ever seemed to change.

I'll always be grateful to Malcolm Glazer and his family for giving the Tampa Bay area its chance to keep the franchise during our stadium debate in 1996. Without the referendum that passed and led to the construction of Raymond James Stadium, there's no doubt the franchise would've been forced to move.

As a franchise, we turned the corner by hiring Tony Dungy, sticking to the plan of developing our own players, and getting the new stadium built. Pretty soon, our players started making the Pro Bowl. The Bucs were on magazine covers and national television. We got mentioned practically every year as a Super Bowl contender. Then Jon Gruden, one of the most driven men I've ever been around, came aboard in 2002 and helped push us over the top to win a Super Bowl championship.

I felt great for the fans. It was nice to see them genuinely excited and genuinely proud of the franchise. Those folks went through a lot, and they had finally reached the end of the rainbow.

Now I have a new role as president and general manager of the Atlanta Falcons. That doesn't change my feelings toward the Tampa Bay area or the franchise that really shaped so much of my adult life. The franchise continues to be the rallying point of the area and there are no fans more loyal than those who follow the Bucs. History—both the good and the bad, and there has been plenty of both—has proven that.

Tales from the Bucs Sideline. The title is perfect.

This franchise—believe me, I know—has stories to tell.

—RICH MCKAY
Former General Manager of the Tampa Bay Buccaneers and current President/General Manager, Atlanta Falcons

INTRODUCTION

Our original premise was to focus on the Tampa Bay Buccaneers and their fresh 2002 world-championship season. Given the strong personalities and national following the Bucs established while seizing the NFL's kingdom, that was a worthy tale in itself.

The Bucs won Super Bowl XXXVII in dynamic fashion. One of the greatest defenses in NFL history mashed the favored Oakland Raiders and their top-ranked offense 48-21, placing the success-starved Tampa Bay area at the center of the sports universe.

A look at the team's most celebrated achievement, however, can only be put in historic perspective by revisiting what the franchise had overcome—an era when the Bucs were known as the "Yucks."

"A collection of the greatest stories ever told" would be incomplete by merely chronicling Tony Dungy's righteousness, Warren Sapp's brashness and Derrick Brooks's dominance. The best of times (eight playoff teams and one Super Bowl champion) were unforgettable. So were the worst of times (when the franchise, at its nadir, made the Los Angeles Clippers cringe).

No one can take away that first world title. Just as no one can erase the string of futility that once defined the Bucs. It took a general manager with a plan, the right coach and an owner willing to spend his money to end the mind-numbing ineptitude. The memories, though, will never go away.

• How about 26 straight losses to usher in the franchise?

• Or the wisecracks of Coach John McKay, who oversaw that early misery. Asked what he thought of his team's execution, McKay said, "I'm in favor of it."

• Long before the intimidating pewter and red scheme took NFL Merchandise by storm, the Bucs wore uniforms that were a hideous shade of orange and featured a winking pirate mascot on the helmet.

• The Bucs drafted Auburn running back Bo Jackson first overall in 1986. The Heisman Trophy winner visited Tampa, considered what he was getting into and said, "No way." Instead, he played baseball. Later, he surfaced in the NFL—with the Raiders.

• The Bucs drafted Miami quarterback Vinny Testaverde first overall in 1987. Testaverde threw 35 interceptions his second season—still the second most in league history—amid revelations that he was color blind.

• Quarterbacks Doug Williams, Steve Young and Trent Dilfer were let go. Williams wanted too much money, Young was traded and Dilfer was not re-signed. All three went elsewhere and won Super Bowls as starters.

We can't make this stuff up, folks, but the Bucs eventually made up for all of it, in front of 800 million witnesses worldwide.

This is their story—the Super and not-so-Super.

Actually, these are their stories.

Tales from the Bucs Sideline.

—CHRIS HARRY AND JOEY JOHNSTON

Chapter 1

THE CHAMPIONSHIP SEASON

The Moment

It took cornerback Ronde Barber about 14 seconds to run 92 yards in sub-freezing temperatures, but the impact of his decisive fourth-quarter interception of Donovan McNabb in the NFC Championship Game at Philadelphia was 27 years in the making.

Inside a silenced Veterans Stadium, Barber sprinted upfield—not an Eagle in sight—as realization sunk in.

The Buccaneers, a franchise once bad beyond belief, were going to the Super Bowl.

"It's like that movie, *The Wizard of Oz*," Coach Jon Gruden said. "You know, 'Ding, dong, the witch is dead.'"

Few not wearing pewter and red saw this coming. The Bucs had never won a playoff game on the road, had a history of awful performances in cold weather and were playing at a venue—the hell hole known as "The Vet"—where their previous two seasons had died ugly postseason deaths.

"Run!" General Manager Rich McKay screamed from his seat in the press box, his fist pounding the table. "Don't ever stop running!"

To the players on the field, the sight of Barber's No. 20 shrinking in the distance made them numb, made them humble, made them cry.

On the festive visitors' sideline, three men sought each other out: strong safety John Lynch, defensive tackle Warren Sapp and linebacker Derrick Brooks. With 26 combined seasons as Bucs between them, the origins of which were anything but promising, the trio now had a bird's-eye view of the rest of the NFC.

With one giant hug, the trio claimed their kingdom.

The greatest moment in Tampa Bay Buccaneers history. Cornerback Ronde Barber returns an interception 92 yards to clinch the 2002 NFC Championship Game against Philadelphia. (The Tampa Tribune)

"We've worked so hard for this," they sobbed in unison. "We've worked so damn hard."

The championship season began on the posh fields of Disney's Wide World of Sports complex near Orlando, where Gruden's first training camp set the tone. An ongoing theme was in place long before the fiery coach showed up. Gruden didn't mess with a defense that had defined the team's Sundays years before he arrived.

That defense delivered a once woebegone organization to football's penultimate moment.

"They used to call us the Yucks," Lynch said. "Look at us now."

A Statement in Vick-Tory

Michael Vick. Michael Vick. Michael Vick.

The second-year Atlanta quarterback was all the rage for the better part of the 2002 season. He took a bad Falcons team that began 1-3 and with his rifle left arm and unrivaled escapability reeled off an eight-game unbeaten streak heading into an NFC South showdown against the Bucs. The week before, Vick had passed for 173 yards and rushed for 173 more, including a 46-yard touchdown run to clinch an overtime win at Minnesota.

The Bucs were 9-3, tied for the best record in the NFL, but you wouldn't have known that by the pregame line of questioning which centered on Vick. At one point, Brooks turned to Sapp with an observation.

"He's been hot for eight weeks," Brooks said. "Our defense has been hot for eight years."

Their ascension was built on defense. The club's most significant free agent acquisition had been linebacker Hardy Nickerson. The coach who changed the attitude was Tony

Dungy, a career defensive coordinator. And the team's greatest single-day draft haul came when Sapp and Brooks were taken in the same first round.

It was defense that awakened Tampa Bay in 1997 to its first playoff berth in 14 years. It was defense that got the Bucs to the 1999 NFC Championship Game.

"Defense is our identity," McKay said. "That's not a bad identity to have."

Yet, Tampa Bay's defense seemingly was serving as Vick's warm-up act. This was especially curious considering the Bucs had knocked Vick out of the game in a 20-6 triumph at the Georgia Dome nine weeks earlier. The Falcons hadn't lost since.

Many forecasters figured they wouldn't lose this time.

On the third play of the game, Vick dropped into the pocket. With nothing developing in Tampa Bay's stingy secondary, he decided to take off.

Brooks decided to tee off.

The jarring blow sent Raymond James Stadium into a frenzy and set the tone for what ended up a 34-10 blowout victory. In two games against the Bucs, Vick combined to go 16 of 37 for 162 yards, one touchdown and an interception.

The week of the game, an ESPN.com poll had voted Vick the "the most electrifying athlete in sports," receiving 50.7 percent of the vote, easily out-distancing the likes of Tiger Woods, Mario Lemieux, Allen Iverson, Kobe Bryant, Tracy McGrady and Sammy Sosa.

"All the talk this week was, 'How do you stop Michael Vick?' I didn't hear anybody in America say, 'How's Michael Vick going to attack that defense?'" Gruden said after the game. "We haven't exactly been chopped liver since the beginning of the season."

Better than that, the 2002 Bucs played some of the best defense of all time.

Nowhere to Run

Only five teams in 2002 had worse rushing attacks than the Bucs. Gruden fed the ball to his featured back 204 times, but Michael Pittman managed only 718 yards and one touchdown.

"It's too late in the season to make a bunch of excuses and tell you all the different reasons that we are where we are," Gruden said after his team gained a season-low 34 yards in a 23-20 loss at New Orleans in December. "The bottom line is that is unacceptable and it has put us in some unbelievably difficult situations."

Earlier in the season, in preparing for a game against Minnesota, a reporter went to Gruden and wondered why fullback Mike Alstott wasn't utilized more, reminding the coach he'd be wise to check Alstott's history for big games against the upcoming opponent, the Vikings.

So Gruden did some background work. He found Alstott had a track record against the Vikings. Gruden decided it would be an Alstott day.

It all played out. The Bucs' passing game had its season-best afternoon, as quarterback Brad Johnson completed all but seven of his 31 passes for 313 yards, five touchdowns and no interceptions. With a red-hot quarterback, it only made sense that the Vikings defense would be susceptible to the run. They were. Sort of.

The Bucs rushed 30 times for 133 yards; 59 came on one carry by reserve Aaron Stecker (the longest run by a Tampa Bay back in 2002). Alstott, meanwhile, got a season-high 26 carries ... for 55 yards.

A couple days later, Gruden sought out the wanna-be coach with a question.

"You were right about Alstott," Gruden sneered to the reporter. "So which of those 2.1-yard carries did you like the best?"

Glad to Have Brad

Brad and Nikki Johnson were rolling down Interstate 75 during the offseason, en route from Atlanta to their home in Tallahassee, listening to sports-talk radio.

In NFL news, the Tampa Bay Buccaneers have signed quarterback Rob Johnson, who was released last week by the Buffalo Bills in a salary cap-cutting move. Johnson, who also played for the Jacksonville Jaguars, is expected to compete with incumbent starter Brad Johnson for the Bucs' No. 1 job in new coach Jon Gruden's offense. In other news … .

Johnson eased off the accelerator, pulled off the highway and looked at his wife.

"We laughed," he said.

They'd laughed before. Wherever Brad Johnson had gone, some hotshot was there or on his way. At Florida State, it was future Heisman Trophy winners Charlie Ward and Chris Weinke. At Minnesota, it was future Hall of Famer Warren Moon and three-time MVP Randall Cunningham. At Washington, it was former No. 1 overall draft pick Jeff George. At Tampa Bay, it was hometown hero Shaun King.

Now, it was Rob Johnson.

Whoever. Whatever.

"I've been around great players my whole career," Johnson said during his first Gruden training camp. "All I can do is worry about myself."

When Rob Johnson arrived in Tampa Bay, all the talk focused on how his build, mobility and arm strength closely resembled that of Rich Gannon, the ageless wonder whose career Gruden resurrected in Oakland. Rob Johnson may have had the physical tools, but Brad Johnson had a better understanding of what it took to play quarterback.

With Gruden pulling his strings, Brad Johnson flourished like never before. In fact, no Tampa Bay player grew more in the eyes of Gruden than his unsung veteran. Johnson, who was voted to the Pro Bowl, completed 62.3 percent of his throws for 3,049 yards, 22 touchdowns, and just six interceptions.

But the most telling statistic came when Johnson could not play. Sidelined for three games due to rib and back injuries, the Bucs turned the offense over to Rob Johnson and King. In those three games, the offense produced nine field goals and one touchdown.

Follow the Leader

His team hadn't sniffed the end zone all day. The offense had managed only three field goals and less than 200 yards in nearly 59 minutes in a road game at Carolina. Yet, the score was tied, though you wouldn't have known by the relatively low-key Tampa Bay bench.

That's when Brooks took over.

As if to will his teammates to victory, Brooks went from Buc to Buc—healthy, injured, suited up or not—and ordered each to join forces on the sideline.

"Everybody get up and come and see this win!" Brooks commanded.

Everybody did, because Brooks said so.

Moments later, Bucs spilled onto the field in jubilation as Martin Gramatica sailed a 47-yard field goal through the uprights for a 12-9 road victory over the Panthers.

Brooks was right. More importantly, the real Brooks was back.

In the third game of the 2001 season, Brooks severely sprained his ankle in a win against Green Bay. Though he dared not speak of it, the injury hindered Brooks the rest of the season. He still managed to start all 16 games for a fifth straight season and lead the team in tackles for a fourth straight.

He vowed to return with a vengeance.

The following offseason, Brooks sat out all conditioning workouts and mini-camps until he was certain the ankle had healed completely.

If anyone had any doubt, it vanished in the final seconds of the second week.

With the Bucs trying to nail down their first shutout in two years, the Baltimore Ravens had driven inside the Tampa Bay 5 with just over a minute to go. As quarterback Chris Redman brought his unit to the line, Brooks bounced on his toes, as if the outcome was dependent on the next play, cajoling his teammates to preserve the goose egg. The ball was tipped at the line, Brooks settled under it and raced 97 yards for the second-longest interception return in Bucs' history and a 25-0 final margin.

"I think maybe Derrick Brooks might be all the way back," joked linebackers coach Joe Barry.

The next week, Brooks returned a Kurt Warner interception 39 yards with 59 seconds to play to seal a 26-14 Monday night victory against the St. Louis Rams, yet it was one of his cheetah-like kills of tailback Marshall Faulk early in the game that grabbed Gruden's attention.

"Did you see that?" Gruden asked no one in particular on the sideline.

Gruden mentioned the play to Brooks the next day and was met with a curious look.

"Coach," Brooks said, "I've been doing this for a while."

In 2002, no one played better. Brooks's 170 tackles led the team for the fifth season in a row. He had five interceptions and returned four turnovers for touchdowns. He was honored as the NFL Defensive Player of the Year.

"It's great to get this award, and it's very humbling," Brooks said. "But hopefully we can move beyond all this individual stuff."

The Ghosts and Mr. Muir

Bill Muir was hired to coach the offensive line before the team hired a head coach. Muir agreed to join the Bucs staff in anticipation that Bill Parcells was coming. Muir was Parcells's line coach for three years with the New York Jets.

When Parcells backed out, the Bucs held on to Muir and Gruden was delighted. Muir, 60, inherited a unit that struggled during the 2001 season, finishing next to last in rushing at just 85.7 yards per game while allowing 47 sacks, including 10 in one game. Muir vowed change.

"They won't have a hard time figuring me out," the curmudgeon promised.

By the time training camp rolled around, a combination of free agency and Muir's heavy hand had resulted in a 60-percent unit turnover. Roman Oben, a Cleveland salary cap casualty signed in May, lined up at the crucial left tackle spot, with Kerry Jenkins, a free agent who followed Muir from the Jets, at left guard. Jeff Christy, a starter since joining the Bucs in 2000, returned at center, as did right guard Cosey Coleman. Second-year pro Kenyatta Walker, who started every game his rookie season at left tackle, was switched to the right side.

Scouting reports for the first half of the season were uninspiring, but Muir used his old-school style—complete with Technicolor vocabulary—to mold his unit into overachievers.

"He'd give us 100-word speeches and 95 of them were curse words," Coleman said. "The man comes at you like a hurricane."

Eventually, so would Muir's offensive line.

Mr. Tough Guy

Jenkins suffered a fractured left fibula in a victory against St. Louis in the third game of the season. The next morning, Gruden announced that Jenkins would be out for two to four weeks due to the injury.

"It's a serious blow to our team," Gruden said.

Six days later at Cincinnati, Jenkins started and played the entire game in a 35-7 wipeout of the Bengals. After the game, Jenkins steered clear of any purple-heart chatter. It took a fractured eye socket in Game 9 to finally knock Jenkins out of the lineup, stopping his string of 56 straight starts.

"I don't really want to talk about it," he said. "It's the only way I know how to do it."

Gruden didn't dismiss his player's will so easily.

"I don't know that Kerry Jenkins will be making any Halls of Fame, but he's making mine," Gruden said.

Ugly Hit, Ugly Aftermath

Sapp had the perfect angle to take out Green Bay offensive tackle Chad Clifton. Cornerback Brian Kelly was returning an interception during the Bucs' 21-7 late-November victory—a win that would give Tampa Bay the best record in the NFL at 9-2—when Sapp, with a running start, launched into Clifton's chest. The hit, a good 20 yards from Kelly's return, was so devastating it broke Clifton's pelvis and left him in a Tampa hospital for three nights. It also drew the wrath of Packers Coach Mike Sherman.

Sherman chased down Sapp after the game and accused him of a cheap shot. Sapp, at first, was caught off guard, then went on the offensive.

"Put a jersey on!" a wild-eyed Sapp raged. "You're so bad, put a jersey on!"

The men were separated and left to defend their actions in the postgame locker room. Sapp maintained he'd done nothing wrong. "I can count the number of personal fouls I've had in my career on two fingers. I don't play that way. I know what a clean shot is. Front is front, back is back. I hit him right in the mouth." Sherman was just as upset by what he perceived as a celebratory attitude from the Tampa Bay sideline while Clifton was being attended by team doctors and an ambulance was pulling into the stadium.

Sherman: "I just don't think there's any place in the game for that. Maybe I overreacted to the hit, but what I saw looked kind of cheap. But who knows?"

Sapp: "He's lucky I'm not 25 without kids and a conscience."

Sherman: "The joviality that existed after a guy's laying on the ground, with numbness in his legs and fingers, I just thought that wasn't appropriate for any NFL player. I have a lot of respect for the game, and I just didn't think that was the place for that. We'll look at the tape."

Sapp: "I see a guy going at my man and I put a lick on him. What's the problem? I didn't clip him. I didn't hit him below the waist. There's not a flag on the play. What's the problem here? This is a contact sport. I didn't hit him in the head. Didn't rough anybody or hit the quarterback. I didn't pick anybody up and slam him. What's the problem?"

The incident was the talk of the league the next day, but Sapp's team backed him. Eventually, so did the league, which ruled the hit was legal.

"Hell, it's on the cover of *USA Today*, for crying out loud!" Gruden said. "I don't like that Warren Sapp is thrown into a negative in terms of how he played during that football game. He played with a great work ethic and within the rules, and there's a confrontation after the game that was not initiated by him."

Brooks seconded.

"He wasn't celebrating the big hit. I know Sapp. He is not a dirty player," Brooks said. "I think something that gets lost is that when you make a hit on someone, you don't know if that guy is hurt; you're celebrating the play. What happened after the play, of course, it's sad. But at the time, it's not celebrating hurting someone. And if anyone has that perception, I would have to question that person."

With that, Gruden wanted the focus shifted to what really mattered.

"I'm not going on *Hard Copy* or one of those deals," he said. "It's over. We're moving on."

Great Wasn't Good Enough

Under Dungy and defensive coordinator Monte Kiffin, the Bucs built a reputation as one of the league's elite defensive units. In the five seasons before Gruden arrived, Tampa Bay ranked third, second, third, ninth and sixth in total defense.

That's why it surprised some players when Gruden, hired in great part for his offensive acumen, challenged the defense during his first team meeting.

"John Lynch!" Gruden said, calling out the four-time Pro-Bowl strong safety and team captain. "You're a great player ... but now I want more out of you."

Lynch, at first, was taken aback. Then the message sunk in.

"I loved it," he said.

Gruden wanted more. In some cases, he knew exactly how much more.

"I want nine touchdowns from this defense," he said. "Nine."

By the time the regular season closed, the Bucs had become the first unit since the 1985 Chicago Bears to lead the league in total defense, points allowed and interceptions. Included were two road shutouts, the second a 15-0 beat down of the Bears in a Sunday night season finale. Yet the Bucs had just five defensive touchdowns.

The balance of Gruden's order would be due in the playoffs.

Hairy Tale

Temperature at kickoff for the season finale against the Bears at Champaign, Illinois, was 28 degrees. On that night, the Bucs clinched the inaugural NFC South Division title and broke their enigmatic 0-21 record for games that began below 40 degrees.

After the convincing shutout, keyed by four interceptions, Tampa Bay defensive end Simeon Rice froze the locker room when he emerged wearing an outrageous full-length white fur coat.

As Rice passed a group of reporters, several of whom were interviewing burly center Jeff Christy, one asked where Rice had gotten such a garment.

"It's made of the hair off Christy's back," Rice said.

Everybody but Christy laughed.

Steaming Rice

Laughter in the presence of the affable, witty and oftentimes flighty Rice was not unusual; unless you were the guy assigned to block him. An explosive combination of speed, strength, size, and athleticism, Rice's arrival in 2001—via a risky free agent contract—provided a long-missing element to the Tampa Bay defense.

Rice signed a five-year, $34 million contract with the Bucs, who were pressed tight against the league-imposed salary cap. The deal included no signing bonus and called for Rice to make just $1 million his first season. Rice had to perform now to make his money later.

"And there was never a doubt," he said.

He came from the Arizona Cardinals with a reputation of being weak against the run, not to mention somewhat "out there" with his personality. This was a player who, while staging a holdout, called Arizona "the armpit" of the NFL. Once back with the team, Rice was reminded of his underarm remark.

"That's OK," he said. "I'll be the deodorant."

Though it took half a season to adapt to the Bucs' disciplined defensive front, the moment things clicked for Rice was a frightening epiphany for left tackles. He had 10 sacks in his final nine games.

Though absent from the team's workouts in Gruden's first offseason program, the coach did a double-take when Rice showed up looking like he'd spent the last two months in a weight room.

"I come in ripped up, shredded, chiseled, six pack, all that," Rice said.

Rice led the NFC in 2002 with 15 1/2 sacks and set a league record by getting two or more in five straight games. He forced six fumbles, knocked down 11 passes and had an interception. Weak against the run? Rice led all Bucs defensive linemen in tackles with 75, yet saved his most beastly performances for the playoffs.

Along the way, he brought his A-game to the media, also.

• On missing off-season workouts: "I'm trans-Atlantic. I'm in Europe, L.A., doing my thing. I keep it tight like that."

• On his reputation as an international ladies man: "The only ethnicity I limit myself to is the one known as 'Fine.'"

• On the sky-high expectations of Gruden's first team: "If you are picked to win the whole show and go the distance and be the top dog, the alpha male, and you don't do it, then [people] are true when they say you are overrated."

• On his slow transition to the Tampa Bay scheme: "The defense wasn't decked out for me, it was decked out for Warren, Derrick and other guys. I had to fall into my place, you know what I mean? I'm used to being at the top of the food chain."

• On what he brings to the Bucs defense: "I bring a lot of intangibles. I also bring tangibles."

• On his dime-store poetry: "Eloquent. It's really colorful. It's a better way to see life. It's rich. It builds a picture. I just speak. I let the words fall from my lips. It hits you there and has a magic sound."

• On the play of the 2002 unit: "This defense is cut for my cloth. When they invented this defense I'm sure the Gods of defense were thinking about me."

Some used the term "overrated" to describe Rice when he came to the Bucs.

No one has used it since.

Congratulations! Now What?

The season-ending defeat of Chicago earned the Bucs a first-round bye into the playoffs. The wild-card round saw the NFC

West champion San Francisco 49ers beat the New York Giants in a wild 39-38 shootout, sending the Niners east for Tampa Bay's first home playoff game in three years.

It wasn't close.

The Bucs jumped on the Niners for three second-quarter touchdowns and coasted to a 31-6 triumph, as the Tampa Bay defense silenced Terrell Owens and his pom-poms by holding the league's eighth-ranked offense to just 228 yards.

Yet even after one of the biggest victories in team history, skeptics wondered what sort of doom awaited the Bucs in their third NFC title shot. The opponents were the Eagles and the venue was the dreaded Vet, set to host its final football game.

Gruden was asked how the Bucs would deal with the cold-weather foe.

"Jiminy Christmas! Philadelphia is in America now," an annoyed Gruden said. "We're not going across the world. It's only a two-hour, 12-minute flight ... and we're going."

Gruden's declaration wasn't needed to fire up the Bucs. They knew what was at stake. All the promise of previous seasons had been washed away with no-shows at Philadelphia. Their most lopsided defeat of the regular season was a 20-10 thrashing in which the offense went touchdown-less for a third straight trip to the Vet.

It was a chance for a breakthrough.

"You want to be considered one of the great teams to ever play this game," Sapp said. "Our stats say we are. But our fingers don't say we are."

NFC Champs and a Guy Named Joe

It took one play from a most unlikely hero. Wide receiver Joe Jurevicius, who missed the entire week of practice due to complications with his newborn son, caught a short slant on a third and three from the Tampa Bay 24 and sped 71 of the most invigorating yards in team history. All the way to the Philly 5.

"The play ignited our sideline," Lynch said. "It told us, 'This is our game.'"

The Bucs, who scored on Alstott's one-yard run to pull ahead 10-7, would not trail the rest of the way. A touchdown pass from Brad Johnson to Keyshawn Johnson and a second-half field goal from Martin Gramatica built the 10-point cushion heading into the fourth quarter.

McNabb, the quarterback who had dazzled the Bucs in three previous meetings, gave the home crowd hope by driving the Eagles to the Tampa Bay 12 with four minutes to go. Wideout Antonio Freeman was open for a millisecond, but Barber saw it all developing.

Just like that, ball in hand, Barber saw nothing but green between himself and something most players only dream about.

The gasp of the crowd was drowned out by the glee of the defiant Bucs.

On the sideline, Gruden triumphantly pumped his fist in the air. Players whooped and hollered. Coaches embraced.

"This is the greatest day of my life," Gruden would say afterward.

In the press box, the son of the team's first coach jumped to his feet and screamed for Barber to run faster, as if something might go wrong.

"I guess you're not supposed to do that in the press box, yelling and screaming ... but wow!" McKay said. "When it becomes real, and you know it's actually going to happen, you think of so many things."

In the owner's box, Executive Vice President Joel Glazer, son of the owner who reshaped one of the shoddiest organizations in pro sports, launched his body into family members. Eight years earlier, everybody laughed at Malcolm Glazer when he spent

$192 million—a record price for a sports franchise—on a perennial loser.

Last laughs are priceless.

"That picture in my brain, No. 20 going the other way, will be with me the rest of my life," Joel Glazer said.

As it will for every Bucs fans.

Tampa Bay 27, Philadelphia 10.

The scene of the defense's three stalwarts was magical.

"It was the longest hug I've ever been a part of," Lynch said. "Me, Sapp and Brooks have been on teams where finishing .500 was our Super Bowl. The hug was a culmination."

Around them, teammates soaked in every last drop of vindication.

"To hell with the Vet," Walker, the young lineman, screamed. "We just burned this place down."

In the City of Brotherly Love, hell had frozen over. Back in Tampa, pigs were flying.

The Bucs were going to the Super Bowl.

On the sidelines, Keyshawn Johnson turned to no one in particular. "I don't know whether to laugh, scream, cry or run naked through the street."

Rice, who played one of the greatest games of his life, had ignored the bitter nighttime cold and stripped to his waist. Johnson got his answer.

"Do 'em all."

Meanwhile …

They were dancing in the streets and then some back in Tampa; not that the Bucs could join the celebration. Once back from Philly, they had to leave for San Diego, site of Super Bowl XXXVII, in just over 12 hours.

And as if Gruden needed any more motivation, he learned during the return flight that the Oakland Raiders, his former team, had soundly beaten the Tennessee Titans 41-24 for the AFC title.

For nearly a year, Gruden had been reminded of the exorbitant compensation package—two first-round draft picks, two second-rounders and $8 million—the Bucs surrendered to pry him from his contract.

"I'm very sensitive to that," he said more than once.

Gruden's patience was about to be tested a thousand times over. Yes, the price was high.

The payback would be hell.

The Arrival

When the Bucs arrived in sun-splashed San Diego, the scene turned surreal. It was Media Day at Qualcomm Stadium. Thousands of reporters, cameramen and hangers-on roamed the field, looking for insight from Tampa Bay's stars, backups and anyone standing still.

During Keyshawn Johnson's mass interview session, a Don King impersonator interrupted. Keyshawn winced. "Can we get a real reporter, please?" he said.

McKay was sought for perspective. "It was a slow boat to China, and the boat had holes," he said on the franchise's interminable climb to respectability.

But no one enjoyed the proceedings more than Sapp, who wore his shades and a broad smile. Besides the game itself, this was the greatest moment for Tampa Bay's often loquacious and outrageous player.

"My body is buzzing all over," Sapp said. "I'm in new ground, uncharted waters. I always watched Media Day. You'd see Emmitt [Smith] with the shades on. You'd watch Leon Lett sit up here for 15 minutes, doing nothing but sweat. I was thinking, 'What if I pulled a Leon Lett today? What if I sat here and just said nothing?' Then I thought about wearing an eyepatch. Hey, you've got to have fun with this."

Most of the Bucs were in their glory. Not Gruden. The media activities were cutting into his preparation. Most of the questions he wanted to avoid.

What are your emotions facing your former players?
Why did you want to leave Oakland?
What's it like taking two teams to the same Super Bowl?

For the most part, the Raiders tackled the same queries. But while Gruden tap-danced his answers, the Raiders stomped.

When Jonny Comes Marching Home

Even before the Super Bowl became official, Gruden was asked about the possibility of a Bucs-Raiders game. He tried (unsuccessfully) to downplay that angle.

"It's a sidebar," Gruden said. "Maybe Section D, Page 19, lower right-hand column. I tried to go quietly. I have a lot of respect for where I came from."

Gruden heard otherwise after his departure. Some players essentially said good riddance. One of them was wideout Tim Brown, a team captain, who claimed the former coach created an overly tense atmosphere.

"Four years and he never says a negative word," Gruden said. "Everything is roses. Then you leave and all of a sudden, you are what you are. The biggest plague to come into this building. It's nice to know, I guess. It hurts. It does hurt."

When Super Bowl week commenced, Raiders offensive tackle Lincoln Kennedy fired more salvos.

"He wants to rule the world," Kennedy said, after accusing Gruden of having a Napoleonic complex. "I'm 6-foot-7. He's 5-foot-nothing. He has this little scrunch on his face when you are around him. He takes little shots at you. It's funny. I laugh every time I see him. He's not mean in any way. For me to try to look at him when he is trying to be big and bad is hilarious."

More Kennedy: "I think he [Gruden] likes having the attention. He likes being part of the camera. That's just the type of person he is. Nothing wrong with it. It's just tickling to me to see someone of his stature act like that."

And this from wide receiver Jerry Porter: "When Gruden left, I breathed a sigh of relief. He created an uptight atmosphere around the practice facility and meetings. Coach [Bill] Callahan is more laid-back and lets things happen."

Any wonder Gruden couldn't wait for kickoff?

Pound That Rock! Literally

The oldest Bucs player at the Super Bowl was 39-year-old back-up tackle Lomas Brown. The exact age of the oldest member of the team, however, could not be determined.

"Anywhere from 400,000 to 20 million years," said Dr. Pat Abbott, geology professor at San Diego State University.

No one knew if it was limestone, granite or what, but the 80-pound rock that showed up in the Bucs' locker room one day during the season took on an identity all its own. It was the brainstorm of defensive line coach Rod Marinelli and it gave new meaning to one of Gruden's favorite sayings: "Pound that rock!"

Said Coleman: "You keep pounding the rock and pounding the rock and pounding the rock, sooner or later, it's going to crack," Coleman said. "That's how we do our business. That's why we're in the Super bowl."

The rock made the trip, too. In more ways than one.

"The rock is always right here," Marinelli said, pointing to his head and patting his chest. "It's in your heart and in your mind."

Gruden: Questions, No Answers

By week's end, Gruden had wearied of talking about his old team.

"This has been a real strange week for me," he said. "Some of these questions are almost impossible to answer without making somebody mad. The only thing I can say is I'm so happy for a lot of those people there. At the same time, I can't tear myself in half with all these emotions.

"I don't know about bitterness. It's a profession where players and coaches change teams. I don't live in a rear-view mirror. I heard Bill Parcells say one time that he is not for everybody and I know that's for sure with me, too."

Gruden said the last time he had spoken with Raiders managing general partner Al Davis, it was the night when the trade was made that shipped his rights to the Bucs.

On Super Bowl game day, Gruden sprinted onto the field. Straight ahead stood Davis. Gruden's Raider tradition was a handshake and small talk with the owner. Gruden debated reviving the ritual, then thought better of it.

Instead, the teams warmed up, as Gruden and Davis, some 20 yards apart, neither spoke nor acknowledged one another.

The gamesmanship was on.

The game was next.

The Game

Super Bowl XXXVII marked the first time in the game's history that the No. 1-ranked offense (Oakland) faced the No. 1-ranked defense (Tampa Bay). The Raiders had Gannon, NFL Most Valuable Player, at quarterback and the league's prolific passing attack, with the incomparable Jerry Rice and Brown at receiver.

Tampa Bay's strategy: Force the Raiders to pass.

"They can say that all they want," Porter said, "but they don't mean it."

Yes, they did. With Gruden's vast knowledge of the Raiders personnel and offensive system, the Bucs had a blueprint to defend Oakland's downfield attack. On the Thursday before the game, Gruden benched his scout team quarterback in favor of himself.

Yes, himself.

There was Gruden, under center, staring down the barrel of Sapp, Brooks and the NFL's best defense.

"I was extremely sharp in there," Gruden said.

Much sharper, it turned out, than the real thing.

On a day the Raiders gained just 19 yards rushing, it was incumbent on Gannon to decipher what the Bucs were doing. Unfortunately for Gannon, the Bucs played as if Gruden had been hiding in the Raiders huddle.

Every subtlety, every seam route, the Bucs were there. An early turnover put Tampa Bay in a 3-0 hole, but free safety Dexter Jackson got in Gannon's head with a pair of first-half interceptions on back-to-back possessions. The first set up a go-ahead field goal, while the second was a key momentum-turner with field position. After the two teams swapped punts, the Bucs needed only to drive 27 yards for a two-yard touchdown run by Alstott and a 13-3 lead.

When Brad Johnson fired a five-yard touchdown pass to Keenan McCardell with 34 seconds to go before intermission,

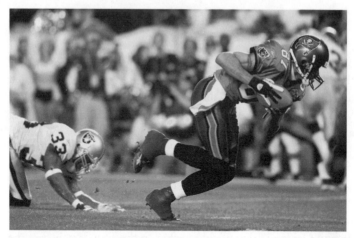

Bucs wide receiver Keenan McCardell beats Oakland defensive back Anthony Dorsett for a touchdown in Super Bowl XXXVII. (The Tampa Tribune)

the Bucs had a 20-3 lead, and everybody in the house knew what the Raiders, who gained just 62 yards in the first half, had to do in the second half.

"We never thought we'd come out and dominate them and shut them down, but that's pretty much what we did," Sapp said. "And once we dig, we drag you in and then pour dirt on you."

The second half was the burial. After forcing a three-and-out on the first series, Tampa Bay marched 89 yards in 14 plays, with Johnson hitting a wide-open McCardell from eight yards to take a 27-3 lead.

Two plays into Oakland's next possession, a prophecy came true. With Tampa Bay's defensive front teeing off and its secondary locked on Raiders receivers, Gannon was reduced to settling for sideline routs. Nickelback Dwight Smith had announced earlier in the evening, "I'm gonna get me one of those."

He would do better than that. Smith's 44-yard interception return made the score 34-3 with just under five minutes to play in the third quarter.

Oakland managed to score three consecutive touchdowns, missing two-point conversion attempts on each, to close the gap to 34-21 with barely six minutes left. The Raiders had a chance for more until Gannon's pass across the middle hit Brooks in the numbers. He rumbled untouched 44 yards for the game- and championship-sealing touchdown.

Coming off the field, Brooks sobbed a lifetime's worth of emotion, as teammates mobbed their captain. One of the greatest defenses in league history—along with a highly motivated coach—had vindicated itself in the only fashion that mattered.

The result was one of the most devastatingly complete performances in Super Bowl history. The passing game that was so efficient in the first two playoff games remained hot, but it was Pittman's season-high 124 yards rushing that really got the Raiders' defense off balance. On the other side of the ball, the Bucs held the Raiders to 269 yards while forcing five turnovers behind a pass rush that sacked Gannon five times. Simeon Rice, with two of those sacks, was virtually unblockable all day, and was one of several defenders worthy of MVP honors.

And as if to hammer home the point, Smith intercepted yet another pass by Gannon with just 12 seconds to play—and took it for a touchdown, too. Gruden ran down the sideline, paralleling Smith almost the entire 50 yards.

For the Bucs' defense, it was their ninth touchdown of the season.

Take that, Coach.

Take that, Raiders.

Tampa Bay 48, Oakland 21.

The Podium

Amid a rainstorm of confetti, Malcolm Glazer extended his arms into the California sky over and over.

"We were waiting for the right man," Glazer said. "Jon Gruden came from heaven, and now he's taken us to heaven."

Gruden, at 39 the youngest coach ever to win a Super Bowl, hoisted the Lombardi Trophy.

"By God," Gruden said. "This night belongs to Tampa Bay!"

It was a mantra the mighty little coach clinged to the rest of that glorious night.

"Let's get this straight," he ordered. "This is about the Tampa Bay Bucs winning a world championship. This is about our area getting to celebrate. Don't make it about me."

The Day After

Jackson's two early interceptions garnered him MVP honors for the game, but it was Johnson, who threw two touchdown passes, who got the invitation to Disneyland. Jackson had to settle for a new Cadillac Escalade and NFL immortality.

"I'm a little disappointed," Jackson joshed during the day-after news conference. "I always wanted to hang out with Mickey Mouse and the guys, but that's fine. I can ride by Disneyland in my new Cadillac. I'll toot my horn, then I'll go to Six Flags or somewhere."

Gruden, his championship less than 12 hours old, talked of soaking it in.

"The next few days, we're going to go to some parades, man," he said. "I've worked hard long enough. It's time to have some fun. I'm going to go see the water in Florida and relax a little bit. We all deserve that."

About an hour later, as the team bus idled in the hotel parking lot waiting to take the Bucs to the airport, Gruden sat in the front seat bent over paperwork.

It was the off-season conditioning schedule.

In the months that followed, Gruden swore he never cheated the moment. He'd grown up watching the Yankees mob each other after each pennant, Magic Johnson leap into Kareem Abdul-Jabbar's arms after each championship, and Tiger Woods pump a fist after each major.

So Gruden reveled in the team's victory parade down Bayshore Boulevard, appeared on *Late Night With David Letterman* and rang the morning bell at the New York Stock Exchange. It was great to be king.

"The thrill of victory at the highest, man, that's what we're in it for," he said. "That's what it's all about. We're not here for Liberty Bowl watches and Peach Bowl rings. Every year there's a game you got to get to—and you got to win it."

Chapter 2

THE JON GRUDEN ROLLERCOASTER

Fire the %&^#@% Cannons!

The Bucs were into their first training camp under Coach Jon Gruden when the team, choked in the central Florida heat and humidity, got a vintage "Chucky Doll" moment.

Gruden suddenly stopped drills and summoned his struggling offense into a huddle.

"Look up there!" Gruden screamed, pointing toward a corner of the field.

Brad Johnson, Mike Alstott and the rest looked, but saw only blue sky and fluffy white clouds. It didn't take long for them to understand.

"See that [expletive] pirate ship?" Gruden railed. "See those guys up there? They want to fire the [expletive] cannons! If we don't execute and get in the red zone, they can't do their [expletive] jobs! So let's put those guys to work and get in the [expletive] red zone, all right? Let's [expletive] go!"

Never mind that training camp was in Orlando, nor that said pirate ship—a distinctive landmark of Raymond James Stadium in Tampa, with cannons that fire when the Bucs penetrate an opponent's 20-yard line—was about 100 miles away.

The players figured it out.

Not that Gruden was a tough read. His reputation preceded him, along with the hefty price the Glazer family paid the Raiders to attract one of the brightest lights in coaching.

Here's the Deal

On Februray 16, 2002, a Saturday afternoon, Tampa Bay executive vice presidents Joel and Bryan Glazer flew to California, presumably to bring back San Francisco's Steve Mariucci as their head coach. A meandering search for the replacement for fired Tony Dungy was into its fifth week and sixth candidate.

Bill Parcells had stunned the Glazers by dropping out when a deal seemed done. Follow-up candidates Norv Turner and Mike Mularkey, a pair of respected offensive coordinators, were nudged out in favor of Baltimore defensive coordinator Marvin Lewis, the choice of General Manager Rich McKay. The Glazers, however, nixed Lewis after a face-to-face meeting and took over a search process that also included a chat with University of Maryland Coach Ralph Friedgen.

All signs pointed to Mariucci, who was seeking a new deal in San Francisco. Despite leading the team to three playoff appearances in five years, Mariucci was never embraced by management. The Niners agreed to let him speak to other clubs and the Bucs were the first. Potential compensation to pry Mariucci from the remaining two years of his contract was agreed on by the two teams before the Glazer brothers headed west to bring home their man.

Three days later they returned.

With Gruden.

It was one the wildest turns of events in franchise history, with a transaction sealed and a contract signed in the middle of the night. In the past, the Bucs were certain to screw up such circumstances.

But the day Gruden, one of the hottest coaches (and faces) in all of football, came to town, those crazy creamsicle times—like Star Wars—seemed a long, long time ago, in a galaxy far, far away.

In the Still of the Night

When most of the country was in its fourth stage of R.E.M., Joel Glazer was altering the direction of his franchise.

The Glazers spent Sunday afternoon interviewing Mariucci, who was coming off a 12-4 season with the Niners. They were impressed with the affable "Mooch," yet sensed a reluctance to uproot. Mariucci, in fact, spoke of coming to Tampa Bay by himself and leaving his family in San Jose for a year so his youngest son could graduate from high school.

The Glazers were in tune with his hedging and felt it was critical to cover themselves or else run the risk of another humiliating chapter to an already comical coaching search.

Ten days earlier, the Bucs had called Raiders owner Al Davis. He and Gruden's agent were at odds over the team's refusal to extend Gruden's contract past the one year remaining. Though Gruden was the only coach in the NFL to lead his team to divisional titles in two straight seasons, the final year of his contract called for a $1.2 million salary that rated among the bottom third in the league. Gruden's agent, Bob LaMonte, announced his client would not re-sign with the Raiders.

The move was intended as a power play. Either Davis could listen to offers or run the risk of losing Gruden in a year and get nothing.

When the Bucs put feelers out to Davis initially they were told that Gruden would cost Tampa Bay four first-round draft picks and defensive tackle Warren Sapp.

Those conversations were brief.

This time, when Joel Glazer phoned Davis at 11 p.m Sunday, the Bucs had some leverage.

"We're close with Steve Mariucci," Glazer told Davis. "But I want to take one more shot."

Within two hours, the two sides had agreed on compensation: Two first-round picks, two second-rounders and $8 million.

Davis called Gruden at 1 a.m. His wife, Cindy, answered, handed the phone to her husband, and eyed the bedside clock.

"This better be good," she said.

It was.

"Do you want [to go to] Tampa Bay?" Davis asked.

Gruden went from asleep to in shock. Twenty years earlier, an 18-year-old Gruden had spent many a day at One Buc Place while his father worked as running backs coach for Tampa Bay Coach John McKay. His father, a regional scout with the 49ers, and mother had settled just a couple miles north of Bucs headquarters.

"Look, my family lives there," Gruden explained.

Davis listened.

"It's your decision."

Within minutes, Gruden was on the phone with Glazer.

"We have to hammer this out tonight," Glazer said.

By 5:30 a.m., a five-year, $17.5 million deal had been struck. Just in time for the sun to come up.

Two hours later—too excited to be tired—the Glazers spoke to Mariucci. They told him they could sense that his heart wasn't in the move and that they'd already broken off in a new direction.

Mariucci was impressed by the foresight, saying, "You guys read me really well."

They played Davis even better. Oh, sure, the price was a steep one. In time, it would be worth it.

Heeeeeeeeeeeere's Jonny!

In 1992, Green Bay Coach Mike Holmgren dispatched a Packers offensive assistant to pick up his agent at the airport. When the 28-year-old Gruden arrived and greeted his passenger with a, "Hi, Mr. LaMonte," the first thing that struck the agent about the freckle-faced kid with the blonde hair and blue eyes was, "Does this guy have a driver's license?"

Later that day, Holmgren and LaMonte were riding in the back seat when Holmgren made this bold statement: "See that guy up there? He's going to be a head coach in the National Football League one day."

LaMonte was thoroughly confused.

"Who? The driver?"

Holmgren flashed a confident smile.

"That guy is un-be-lieve-able!"

A year later, Gruden was promoted to receivers coach. Two years later, in 1995, he went to Philadelphia and at 31 became the youngest offensive coordinator in the NFL. In 1998, the 34-year-old Gruden became the league's youngest head coach when he joined a Raiders franchise coming off a 4-12 season.

During his first training camp in charge, Gruden called LaMonte and told him he was going to start little-known quarterback Donald Hollas.

"I just thought he meant in a scrimmage," LaMonte said.

The Raiders went 8-8. A year later, Gruden tabbed reclamation project and journeyman Rich Gannon as his starter. Gannon threw for more than 3,800 yards and 24 touchdowns, as Oakland went 8-8 again, setting the franchise up to take its place among the upper echelon of AFC clubs. Gruden would be there for AFC West titles in 2000 and 2001.

He was on the opposite sideline when the Raiders reached the Super Bowl in 2002.

Doll Face

Harvey Williams was a backup tailback for the Raiders in 1998. Midway through the season, Oakland was hosting Seattle, a team that relied heavily on weak-side blitzes. Gruden came up with a special audible for his quarterback, Hollas, to check to when the Seahawks were about to bring an extra rusher from the weak side. "Seattle 96" meant the running back would take a handoff and head for the strong side.

That day, Williams thought he heard "Seattle 97." When Hollas turned for the handoff, there was no running back. The outcome was predictable. So was Gruden's reaction.

Asked about the encounter later, Williams said his coach's rage reminded him of Chucky, the murderous slasher doll in the campy *Child's Play* horror films.

Williams had no idea what he had started with that comment.

When photos of Gruden's incomparable grimace were placed alongside photos of the evil, freckle-faced Chucky, the resemblance was uncanny.

"You should see me when I shank my 4-iron," the coach said.

The intensity of Bucs coach Jon Gruden has become a constant on Tampa Bay's sideline. (The Tampa Tribune)

Chucky dolls became fixtures at Raiders games, and followed Gruden when he came to Tampa. Cameras were assigned by networks to focus solely on Gruden and his expressions.

"I never meant for these faces of displeasure, discomfort, irritation, or whatever you want to call them, to become a sidebar to the game," Gruden said. "What can you say? I'm an animated guy."

At his first Bucs training camp, held in Orlando, Gruden posed for a picture with a kid made up like Chucky. Then he went and verbally hacked a few players on the field.

Work Is His Scripture

Jon 3:17.

To some it might be a Bible verse (minus the "h").

To Gruden, it was—and still is—the most important part of the day.

The start of it.

"It's not scripture," Gruden said. "It's not my lucky lottery numbers. It's not my favorite area code."

So what is it?

"I like to get up early. I can function without much sleep," said Gruden, who first started rising at his ungodly hour during his early days in Oakland. "I wish there was some kind of special significance to it, but there's not. I kind of gauge it on being at the office at a certain time, like quarter after four. After three years in Oakland, I kept going with 3:17 and that's what it's been ever since. It's just a number."

Maybe, but it's become a way of life. Gruden wakes, waits for the paperboy, then stops at his regular convenience store to drink a coffee and read the morning news.

He is most content at a time when most people would be miserable. For him, there is nothing better than settling into his cracker box-sized office, with the first of the day's doses of caffeine, a lone light emanating from the computer screen, and the clock showing 4:15 a.m.

"I like to get in there when it's nice and dark and quiet, with no disturbances," he said. "It gets my mind right for the day ahead. It's not for everybody, I know that. But it's for me. That's how I work."

The Bride of Chucky

Jon Gruden and Cindy Brooks met in 1986 in Knoxville, Tennessee, about 15 miles from her hometown of Sevierville. Cindy was a University of Tennessee cheerleader while Jon was working as a graduate assistant. They bumped into each other around the athletic building. Cindy was the first to bring up the idea that they go out on a date.

"We fell in love in two weeks," she said.

Materialistic they weren't.

They'd go to dinner. He'd talk big. Then the check would come.

"Got any money?" he'd ask.

They married in 1991.

"This guy was going places and I wanted to go with him," Cindy said. "He was so driven and dedicated, and I just loved that about him. Because we dated for so long, I made sure I knew what I was getting into. I'm pretty flexible, pretty independent. I think that's a big part of why it works."

She needs to be all those things to deal with Jon's quirks. This is a guy who can't stand to hear spoons rattle cereal bowls; who will ask people not to snap their bubble-gum; or get up and change seats, sometimes three or four times, in a movie theater if someone is talking.

"That's just Jon," she said.

At home, Cindy handles their three boys, Jon II (who goes by "Deuce"), along with Michael and Jayson. Though he's not home much, sometimes Jon tries to make up for it with flowers and cards, or maybe just a note that says, "I love you."

One of the best things this husband likes about his wife?

"I don't ask him anything about football," said Cindy.

Great move, but nowhere as great as the one Jon pulled off to land his better half. Leave it to the coach to put his marriage in the proper perspective.

"Key acquisition, marrying a woman like that," he said.

A Whole New Scene, Whole New Attitude

When the horn sounded and called to order Gruden's inaugural Tampa Bay mini-camp, the new coach was hopping from hashmark to hashmark, screaming to be heard above the jets that thundered down the nearby airport runway, barking instructions in a voice that dominated his first practice.

Let's get going! Gotta run, really run! Be smoke out there, man!
The pace was as furious as it was fascinating.

"Things were moving pretty fast," Alstott said. "I liked it."

Alstott's initial assessment was not meant as an indictment of the previous coach. Dungy's low-key demeanor defined the winningest era in team history. Gruden's in-your-face methods would define what was to come.

"I think players at this level deserve organization," Gruden said. "They expect a brisk tempo and not a lot of wasted time."

Players sprinted from station to station, with the air horn serving as their timekeeper. Midway through the morning workout, the horn began to fade when Gruden was just getting warmed up.

"Get another horn!" he wailed.

The most significant difference was the tempo on offense. Plays were called in rapid-fire succession. Holdovers from the Dungy regime estimated the Bucs were running 70 plays in the time it used to take to run 40.

And the position meetings were equally frantic.

"Jon's going to talk to you in class, then he's going to repeat it, then he's going to come out here and tell you before the huddle, then he's going to talk you through the play and talk to you after the play," Johnson said. "You're going to hear it five or six times, then go back and watch film and hear it again. He wants you to know the evolution of the play, the history of the play and how defenses have changed for the play."

Added Gruden: "You don't just draw Xs and Os. Bring them out here and teach. You have to sell your system."

After the first workout, Gruden was asked about the malfunctioning horn—specifically, about the guy in charge of sounding it.

"Hopefully," Gruden said, "he's on his way to Wal-Mart right now."

Rising Star

LaMonte's office in Nevada was inundated with endorsement and marketing opportunities for the coach of the Super Bowl champions.

"People want to see Jon Gruden," LaMonte said.

But just as before the world championship, the best place to catch a glimpse of Gruden post-championship was behind his desk.

Despite a persona that took on rock star proportions, Gruden went back to his dark football cave.

"I've got my own deal going and nothing about me is going to change," Gruden vowed in the days leading up to the '03 mini-camp. "If I were to start walking around like I'm some hot [stuff] big shot—I know a few guys in town who'll come out here, kick my ass and toss me in a dumpster off Dale Mabry Highway. I ain't changing."

Out of Key

The combination of Gruden's youth and edgy demeanor gave him a different perspective when it came to dealing with players. His energy was infectious and certainly lit flames under the Raiders and Bucs. But his exit from Oakland, coupled with the fact that he never stopped by to bid farewell to his players, fostered some resentment.

Yet, it was nothing like the mutual antipathy that manifested itself between Gruden and flamboyant wide receiver Keyshawn Johnson.

"I'm a West Coast guy," Johnson said when explaining his routine absences from the club's off-season workouts that Gruden considered anything but voluntary. "I have family and business out there. That's where I'll be most of the off season. All my coaches have understood that."

All but one.

While grizzled pros like Sapp, Derrick Brooks and Brad Johnson sweated through perfect attendance, the team's featured wideout—coming off a 106-catch, Pro Bowl season—showed up only for mandatory mini-camps and stayed away from all off-season work.

Publicly, Gruden tolerated Johnson's non-attendance. Privately, he fumed.

Johnson relished the role of a defiant star. The friction between he and Gruden would be an ongoing theme, even as Johnson caught 76 passes for 1,088 yards and five touchdowns, and he also led the team in catches and yards in the playoffs.

Monday Night Football cameras caught Johnson blowing up on Gruden after the coach kept Johnson on the sidelines for a crucial third-down passing situation against St. Louis. Both men played down the incident for the press.

"I love Keyshawn Johnson," Gruden said. "He's an emotional guy, and so am I."

"I enjoy playing for him. He gets me going," Johnson said. "And I think as time goes by, he'll really start to feel what I can be and do out there."

Time went by, but Gruden and Johnson had learned everything they cared to about each other. To Gruden, Johnson was an overpaid, self-promoting role player. To Johnson, Gruden was a camera-seeking glory hound who wanted all the credit for the Super Bowl run.

"There are no stars on this team," Johnson said during 2003 training camp. "The only star on this team is the coach—and don't you forget that."

Long after the championship buzz had given way to a new season, both men had worn on each other so much that there was no hiding the frayed relationship. In October, the struggling Bucs were preparing to play the Dallas Cowboys, led by Parcells, who had coached Johnson for three seasons with the Jets. In the days leading up to the game, Johnson was asked to name the best coach he'd ever had.

"I'd have to say Bill Parcells."

Four days later, as if to hammer home the point, Johnson was introduced before the home crowd, sprinted from the tunnel, slapped hands with his teammates and rushed to the Dallas sideline to shake Parcells's hand. The crowd booed.

In a 16-0 win that day, Johnson caught one pass. It was on a scramble play and it went for a seven-yard touchdown, but it hardly quenched the receiver's thirst for action. Johnson was the third option on the play.

In the postgame locker room, Johnson clearly was irritated.

"It is what it is," he said. "I don't have to justify myself. I run routes, I block, I do whatever they want me to do."

Gruden was asked about Johnson's role after the game.

"Keyshawn's our first option on every play," said the coach, breaking into a smirk.

Then he left the room.

The Unraveling

As tough and determined as the Bucs were en route to that long-awaited 2002 championship, they defended it with all the conviction of a modern-day French army.

Gruden was hardly blameless.

In fact, the source of the meltdown could be traced to the NFL owners meetings, held two months after the Super Bowl in Phoenix. It was there—in the lobby and gift shop, on the golf course or from a bar stool—that Gruden surprised executives, coaches and even reporters by taking verbal jabs at McKay and the Bucs' front office. Gruden let it be known that he felt McKay, co-chairman of the NFL's Competition Committee, was putting too much time into league matters and not enough into Bucs matters, and that he was less than impressed by his front office's record in recent drafts.

It wasn't long before Gruden's criticism hit the papers.

Now there was a public problem.

A year earlier, Gruden had come to town prepared to tear the roster apart, only to be squelched by McKay, who believed the roster, with an addition here and there, would be fine. The Bucs made those additions and won a Super Bowl, but a year later everything wasn't fine. And with a Lombardi Trophy in the case, Gruden wasn't going to back off so easily.

He blew a gasket when McKay wouldn't sign Emmitt Smith. He was stunned when the Rams traded a second-round pick for offensive tackle Kyle Turley, a player McKay's staff deemed a bad locker room guy. And the Bucs' own free agents? Everything was moving at a snail's pace, but that was McKay's way. He always let the market settle, always had a long-term plan for the salary cap.

Eventually, both men would shrug off the reports as rumor. They weren't.

"I want everything done now. I can't get over it if it's not done now," Gruden said. "And if it's not done tomorrow and wasn't done yesterday I start to become upset because everything is a crisis."

About a week after the owners meetings, nickelback Dwight Smith, who set a Super Bowl record by returning two interceptions for touchdowns, was arrested after pulling a gun on a man in a road rage incident. Three weeks after that, starting right tackle Kenyatta Walker was jailed for his part in a nightclub fracas in Tampa's Ybor City area. And in June, tailback Michael Pittman, one of the Super Bowl stars, was busted for driving his Hummer into a car carrying his wife, baby-sitter and infant son. Pittman was on probation for domestic violence charges at the time.

The Bucs hadn't played a game, yet off the field they were deep in a hole.

It was a harbinger of things to come.

The Beginning of the End

Martin Gramatica was perfect on all 129 of his extra points in his career. All he had to do was make it 130 and the Bucs would be 2-0. But with the game tied 9-9 and no time on the clock, Carolina defensive tackle Kris Jenkins blew up the Bucs' offensive line, blocked the PAT and helped hand Tampa Bay a 12-9 overtime defeat.

"That's one of those games that come along once in a lifetime," safety John Lynch said.

Oh yeah?

Three weeks later, Dungy brought his Indianapolis Colts to town and hung a comeback for the ages on his former team. Down 35-14 with less than five minutes to play, the Colts rallied to tie the game and won 38-35 on a Mike Vanderjagt field goal in overtime.

Four weeks into the season, the Bucs were 2-2, had been on the wrong end of two of the most inexplicable defeats in league history and had lost three starters to injury.

"The challenge is in front of us, not behind us," defensive end Simeon Rice said. "Everything is not going to go right. Guys are going to get hurt—with some done for the season— but we're going to find a way to use the guys who are here and get it done. Pretty simple."

Simple sounding. In the coming weeks, more players, such as Lynch, would get hurt. Then, in November, the Bucs lost four of five games, each coming after they were either tied or ahead in the fourth quarter.

It was all falling apart.

Throwing Away the Key

Tuesday is usually an off day in the NFL, but in mid-November the Bucs called a news conference to drop a bombshell.

Bye-bye, Keyshawn.

The team announced that Johnson had been deactivated for the remainder of the season, saying he'd become a distraction in the locker room. Johnson had gone to team officials and expressed his desire to leave after the season. The Bucs granted his wish six weeks early.

"For whatever reason, he didn't want to be here," Gruden said. "We've worked hard to get him the football. We want our players to be happy, but unfortunately it has festered for a while. I believe it has affected him."

McKay backed Gruden, despite the ramification's Johnson's release—a $7 million hit—would have on the salary cap.

"His approach to us, to the organization and to the team changed," McKay said. "A lot of mandatory workouts missed, a lot of team functions that are football related were not attended, and it became, in our mind, a problem. One that needed to be addressed."

Johnson had no news conference to address his deactivation locally, though he did about 10 radio and TV interviews for the national press.

"I was never Gruden's guy," Johnson told ESPN. "He never liked me. I told him I'd rather retire than play for him in 2004. But I also told him I wouldn't be a distraction, I wouldn't go to the media with it, and I didn't. I don't know why they [deactivated] me. I was playing hard, I wasn't dogging it."

Another Ridiculous Loss

For nine months, whenever the subject came up, Gruden and McKay shot down any talk of a rift between the coach and general manager.

The relationship, in fact, was so disharmonious that McKay didn't last the season.

The philosophical chasm between the two got so wide that McKay went to Joel Glazer and asked to be released from the final four-plus years of a six-year, $12 million contract. Glazer, citing McKay's long and loyal service to the team, granted his GM permission to look elsewhere and waived any consideration for compensation.

Four days later, McKay was putting on an Atlanta Falcons hat in Flowery Branch, Georgia, and being introduced as president and general manager of one of the Bucs' division rivals.

"I guess this kind of proves that rumors can come true," McKay said. "So I apologize to all those members of the media to whom I've always said that's never the case."

But why? How could a man with 28 years of his life invested in a franchise—one basically founded by his father—call it quits in midstream and just walk away? Admittedly, winning the Super Bowl made the decision easier, but the overriding factor was a clash of ideals between the coach and the man in charge of obtaining personnel.

"It's not appropriate for the GM to constantly be the 'no' guy, it's just not. You don't win that way," McKay said. "The stuff written about boisterous exchanges? I've never had a boisterous exchange with anybody in my life. I wish I was that tough. That's not accurate. What it mainly came down to [is] Jon's vision to build the football team and maintain it was different than mine. I really became uncomfortable as to, 'How do I compromise this? How do I make this work? And how do I build consensus?' In a cap era, to the extent that you make mistakes, you will pay the piper."

Back in Tampa, Gruden tried to deflect talk of McKay's departure, but there was no getting by the perception that the coach had won a power struggle with an executive whose name was synonymous with the franchise.

"I have no desire to be a general manager," Gruden said after helping chase one of the best in the business out of town. "None. Zero."

In another fitting chapter in the inexplicable Bucs story of 2003, McKay's first game as a Falcon was five days later ... at Tampa. Atlanta won 30-28. The loss ended the Bucs' slim playoff hopes and officially made the season a monumental failure. An uninspired 33-13 mail-in defeat at Tennessee the next week finished the Bucs at 7-9, making them just the sixth team in league history to follow a Super Bowl title with a losing record.

"It's been a long journey. An EKG. Up and down," Rice said. "But this is rock bottom. As low as you go. We're going home."

Keyshawn Johnson already was there. He found appropriateness in the Bucs' finish.

"It was difficult to watch," Johnson said. "I feel bad for the players that were there, saddened for them, especially guys like Warren Sapp, Derrick Brooks, John Lynch, Brad Johnson and Keenan McCardell. I feel that they got cheated out of a chance to win another Super Bowl because of the things the head coach—or shall I say, 'Head Coach-Slash-General Manager'—did to disrupt the team in terms of the way he went about things with me and the general manager."

After the season, Johnson via trade found a new home, predictably, with Parcells and the Cowboys. As such, he predicted he and Gruden would one day cross paths.

"We'll be fine," Johnson predicted. "I'll say, 'How you doing? Y'all had a good year, played really good down the stretch. … Congratulations.'"

From Going Home to Sent Home

Six weeks after the season was done, Rice showed up for the Pro Bowl in Hawaii.

He was three days late.

By virtue of his tardiness, Rice missed what NFC Coach Andy Reid deemed important meetings and practices, and also learned upon arrival that there was no room for a traveling companion. Rice didn't take the news well and complained enough to cause what the league considered a "disturbance" in the hotel lobby.

At least that's how the NFL described it to Rice in a letter delivered to his room, two days before the game, informing him he'd been dismissed from the All-Star team. The letter also was critical of Rice for showing up to his first practice earlier in the day with his shoelaces untied.

"This trip is supposed to be fun, supposed to be a reward. I'm like, 'Damn! When did it get so serious?'" Rice said. "You stand next to another guy [on the field] and it's like, 'Take it easy, let's not get hurt.' Now, I got my mother over here telling me my shoes are untied. Sorry, Ma."

Some might say it was a perfect end to a flawed season that—like an untied shoe—began slipping away long before it began. How do you get sent home from a Pro Bowl?

Come to think of it, how does everything so right go so wrong?

Gruden didn't have an answer, only a promise.

"We're gonna fix it."

Hand-Picked Partner

Two weeks after the season, the Bucs again raided the Raiders, hiring Bruce Allen as general manager. Allen was a man of distinguished NFL pedigree whose father, George, was a Hall of Fame coach. In Oakland, he had been an apprentice to Davis and worked alongside Gruden.

Now he took over administration of a franchise rapidly becoming known as "Raiders East." Most importantly, Allen saw eye to eye with Gruden's urgency.

"Now Jon, why don't you come up here and tell everyone if we've met before and if you're going to meddle," Allen said with a sardonic smile at his introductory news conference.

Gruden took the podium.

"There's been a lot of speculation, a lot of stereotyping and a lot of unnamed sources reporting on this particular change," Gruden said. "All I can say to our players and to our fans is that we have acquired a great general manager with a lot of juice and he's going to be relentless."

Inside Allen's new office, the screen-saving slogan, "The Future Is Now," already crawled across his computer. It was a phrase made famous by his father, who loved older veterans, barely tolerated rookies and built teams to win immediately.

"It's broader than the idea that you sign a bunch of old guys because you're going to try to win the next game," Allen explained. "We definitely want to win the next game, but it means much more than that. It means take care of these players and coaches today. After that, the future will take care of itself."

The future of the Bucs has yet to be written.

Their past was like no other in professional sports.

Chapter 3

BEGINNINGS

The Buccaneers Are Born

From the 1967 completion of Tampa Stadium—a structure with two free-standing sides and a capacity of 46,700—through 1973, no other non-league city hosted more NFL exhibition games than Tampa.

After years of lobbying owners and Commissioner Pete Rozelle, Tampa was selected as the NFL's 27th franchise city on April 24, 1974 at a cost of $16 million, beating Phoenix, Honolulu, Memphis and Seattle (later awarded the 28th franchise). Hugh Culverhouse, a Jacksonville tax attorney, would be the owner.

The name of "Buccaneers," reflecting the area's pirate heritage and its Gasparilla festival, was chosen from more than 400 entries in a fan contest. The team was called the Tampa Bay Buccaneers (not Tampa Buccaneers) in anticipation of its regional following.

The front page of The Tampa Tribune *on April 25, 1974, the day after the NFL awarded the Tampa Bay franchise. (The Tampa Tribune)*

By October 1975, Culverhouse had hired his coach—John McKay, winner of four national championships at the University of Southern California. The Bucs were officially underway, but no one suspected how arduous the early going would become.

Off and Running (Sort Of)

The Bucs acquired their first players through a veteran allocation draft they shared with the Seattle Seahawks. McKay and Ron Wolf, the team's vice president of football operations, studied data on approximately 2,000 players and learned who was available only days before the draft. There was a scramble for pertinent information, particularly medical updates.

Seattle led off the 78-player draft with Rams linebacker Ken Geddes, who played three more seasons. Tampa Bay then took Raiders tight end Bob Moore.

"The only reason we took Moore was to trade him for more value," Wolf said. "Then we couldn't trade him. He wasn't wild about being in Tampa. We probably bungled that one up."

Steelers offensive tackle Dave Reavis, the player Wolf *really* wanted, was Tampa Bay's second pick, followed by Colts defensive tackle Dave Pear, an early fan favorite and Pro Bowler in 1978. The Bucs also selected Oilers strong safety Mark Cotney, an instant starter.

Productive selections were rare. Remember Durwood Keeton, Bubba Bridges and Earl Douthitt? They never played a down for Tampa Bay.

Seattle's best pick was cornerback Dave Brown, a first-rounder by the Steelers in 1975. He had 62 career interceptions, tying for fifth best all-time in the NFL upon his retirement. Tampa Bay got production from Reavis and Cotney, a bone-rattling defender who was dubbed "Captain Crunch." Both started for eight seasons.

Cotney wasn't thrilled with his selection by the Bucs. A reporter from his hometown newspaper in Lawton, Oklahoma, called to inform Cotney he was headed to the Tampa Bay Buccaneers.

Cotney's initial reaction: "The Tampa Bay Bucca-whos?"

"I was on a Houston team contending for the Super Bowl," Cotney later said. "Suddenly, I'm one of the castoffs."

Welcome to the NFL

McKay's urgency accelerated after the first practice. "Some of the guys who were projected as starters, they might not have made some of our teams at USC," McKay later said. "That's when it started to dawn on me. This might be a bigger challenge than we expected."

Because the team's training complex was not complete, the first mini-camp was held at Tampa's Leto High School. Groundskeepers weren't informed, though, so the first group of Bucs went through drills in knee-high grass.

One Buccaneer Place, described as "state of the art" by Culverhouse, was located near Tampa International Airport. Noise from training camp workouts often was drowned out by the jets buzzing overhead. The location was convenient. Players who were cut—and there was a revolving door early on—didn't have far to go for the trip home.

McKay knew tremendous work was ahead. But in Tampa, there was optimism as the Bucs approached their first exhibition game against the Los Angeles Rams on July 31, 1976. It was staged at the Los Angeles Memorial Coliseum, site of McKay's USC glory days, making for a built-in storyline.

When the Bucs' charter flight landed, the doors opened and the first man lumbered to the ground as the television cameras rolled. A sportscaster remarked, "They seem old and overweight."

Cameras focused on Jim Selman, the 50-something assistant sports editor of *The Tampa Tribune*, who was part of a media contingent seated closest to the exit door.

The Rams won 26-3, hardly an overwhelming margin. McKay remembered it as a mismatch from the start.

"It was the Christians against the lions," McKay said. "When we were first introduced, our first guy on the field limped noticeably. The second was almost winded by the time he made it to the bench. And the third came out so slow I thought we'd get a delay of game penalty. If it had been a league game, it would have been 100-0."

By the third exhibition, at the neutral site of Jacksonville, the franchise had earned its first victory (Tampa Bay 17, Atlanta 3), although it was merely a practice game.

"Oh, well," McKay said afterward, "another dynasty."

Point Us in the Right Direction

Marching out of the Astrodome locker room, Bucs players and coaches took a wrong turn. Fans kept waiting for the emergence of an expansion team, ready for its first regular-season game. But deep in an endless corridor, the Bucs marched further away from the field, until somebody finally spoke up.

"We're going the wrong way."

They had no idea.

The Bucs had just 108 yards of total offense (and 80 yards in penalties). They punted 11 times. Early on, a pass was dropped in the end zone. A 39-yard field-goal attempt hit an upright. The defense broke under the pressure of consistently long drives.

The Houston Oilers prevailed 20-0, and McKay, who said the Bucs would win more than three games to beat the standard of recent NFL expansion teams, grew testy when reminded of his prediction.

"Has this team here, Houston, ever lost any games?" McKay said. "I believe they've been playing 6,000 years and I don't remember any championships won."

Desperate and Winless

In the home opener, a 23-0 loss to San Diego, the offense displayed little speed and shaky blocking. The Bucs finally scored the following week against Buffalo with three field goals, but fell 14-9. With five minutes to go, the Bucs faced fourth and 10 from the Buffalo 20-yard line. McKay tried to fake a field goal, but the pass gained only nine yards. Game over.

Next was a 42-17 defeat at Baltimore (in which the Bucs took a 3-0 lead, then surrendered 42 unanswered points), followed by a 21-0 blanking at Cincinnati. After five weeks, the Bucs had one offensive touchdown.

Now they were facing a home game against fellow expansion team Seattle, also 0-5. It was dubbed the NFL's Game of the Weak. Both teams realized it was the classic must-win situation.

Flag Day

The 1976 Bucs-Seahawks game will be remembered as "Flag Day" by the fans who endured brutal heat to witness what became a mockery of the NFL's Expansion Bowl. Officials marched off 310 yards in penalties. Forty-one flags were thrown and 35 penalties were assessed (20 to Tampa Bay and 15 to Seattle), two off the all-time NFL record. Each team had eight holding penalties.

The Bucs were penalized on the opening kickoff. They were offsides. Seattle led 13-10 with 42 seconds remaining when the Bucs' Dave Green was summoned for a 35-yard field-goal attempt that probably would have forced overtime. Blocked. (Forgotten footnote: The Bucs were flagged for a personal foul penalty, which was declined.)

The game featured Tampa Bay's first touchdown pass. It wasn't thrown by a quarterback. In fact, it wasn't supposed to be thrown at all.

In the third quarter, Tampa Bay had first-and-goal at the Seahawks' one-yard line. Ed Williams, no gain. Louis Carter, no gain. Carter then tried to leap the middle, but was repelled backward onto his feet.

Staggered, Carter noticed wide receiver Morris Owens standing near the sideline. He hurled a two-handed basketball pass to a startled Owens, who then stepped into the end zone. Presto! The first touchdown pass in Tampa Bay history!

Still, the Bucs were 0-6. Their best chance at victory was gone. Leave it to McKay for some levity.

"Like the fans, I figured at the start of the season we would go 14-0," McKay said. "Then we had the first kickoff and didn't score and I said, 'Well, I'll be damned.' Just give us time, we'll win. I don't know when. I hope it's in this century."

Playing Out the String

Unless they got some luck (doubtful) or the offense drastically improved (also doubtful), the Bucs were looking at 0-14.

Facing hopelessness, the Bucs produced their most inspired effort. Against the state rival Miami Dolphins, before the season's largest home crowd (61,437), the Bucs took it into the final minute before Garo Yepremian's 29-yard field goal with 55 seconds to play rescued the Dolphins 23-20.

Parnell "Paydirt" Dickinson, making his only start, completed his first four passes, including an 18-yard TD to Owens before leaving with an ankle injury. Steve Spurrier came off the bench and responded with his best game in Tampa Bay (13 of 21 for 143 yards and two touchdowns, both to Owens, giving him three for the game).

Afterward, the winning Dolphins were shell-shocked. "This is the low point in Miami Dolphins' history," Miami linebacker Nick Buoniconti said.

As for the Bucs, McKay said, "We're definitely getting better. I hope we don't turn around and fall on our faces."

Jinx. Things got worse.

The Bucs dropped to 0-8 with a 28-19 home loss to the Kansas City Chiefs, perhaps the only remaining opponent that seemed beatable. Said McKay of the growing prospects of ending up 0-14: "We are sure as hell working on it."

McKay fumed following a 48-13 loss at Denver. The Bucs led 13-10 in the third quarter before surrendering 35 points in the final 20 minutes. He lashed out at Broncos offensive coordinator Max Coley—"I hope he got his offensive stats up today and I hope he gets fired tomorrow," McKay said—even though three of Denver's final four touchdowns were scored by the defense off Tampa Bay turnovers. McKay was upset because Denver ran a tight-end reverse and threw a pass in the final minute.

Following a 49-16 loss at Oakland (the eventual Super Bowl champion), the Bucs were headed to Pittsburgh.

As 26-point underdogs.

"It is at times like this we all thank our stars that we do have a sense of humor," McKay said.

Terry Hanratty, the former Steeler, was installed as Tampa Bay's starting quarterback. McKay made the announcement, but added he hadn't told Hanratty. "When he reads about it," McKay said, "maybe he'll leave town."

All in all, not a bad idea. Hanratty completed one pass (for a one-yard loss) in four attempts and the Bucs trailed 28-0 when he was removed for Spurrier. Pittsburgh won 42-0. It could have been much worse.

Playoff-bound New England applied the final insult. The Patriots, leading 24-14 with six seconds to play and the ball on the Bucs' 1-yard line, called time out and allowed Steve Grogan to score his 12th rushing touchdown (an NFL record for quarterbacks). For laughs, Patriots linebacker Steve Zabel was sent in for the extra point, which he made.

Patriots 31, Bucs 14. The capper on an 0-14 season. That's all, folks.

The Grim Aftermath

The inaugural Bucs placed 17 players on the injured-reserve list, including Lee Roy and Dewey Selmon. From training camp until the final game, 140 players wore the Bucs' uniform. "We kept having to play with a guy who had just gotten here," McKay said.

The 0-14 embarrassment was downplayed by McKay, especially when reminded of Seattle's 2-12 record. "That is as repugnant to me as 0-14," McKay said. "I don't want to be a team that keeps winning a few games every year and never goes anywhere. Seattle won two games. Should we throw them a parade?"

In McKay's final meeting with players, he asked how many planned to live in Tampa during the offseason. A few dozen hands were raised. "Please stop at the back on your way out," McKay said. "There's a box of fake noses and moustaches."

As for McKay himself?

"I'll probably take a little time off," he said, "and go hide somewhere."

False Optimism

Tampa Bay's defense, clearly, was much improved in 1977. But after injuries to promising quarterback acquisitions Mike Boryla (who had been to the Pro Bowl) and Gary Huff (a former second-round draft pick), the Bucs were forced to open with rookie Randy Hedberg, an eighth-round pick from tiny Minot (N.D.) State.

Hedberg had thrown a 66-yard touchdown pass in an exhibition against Buffalo, then displayed composure in a 14-0 preseason win against Baltimore.

T-shirts and buttons popped up around Tampa—"Why Not Minot?"

"This is preseason," said Colts cornerback Lloyd Mumphord, injecting some reality. "The Buccaneers could still go zero-and-14 this year."

As predictions go, it wasn't bad.

Familiar Territory

Hedberg's regular-season debut was a nightmarish 13-3 loss at Philadelphia. The Bucs gained just 118 total yards. Hedberg was sacked four times and twice needed to be helped from the field.

Four games into the season, the Bucs still hadn't surpassed the 200-yard mark for total offense and bottomed out against Washington (gaining just 136 yards in a 10-0 defeat that saw the Bucs go one for 16 in third-down conversions and included 11 punts and 10 sacks). By then, Hedberg had vanished from the starting lineup. So had realistic hope of a victory.

When the offense finally moved, the defense collapsed in a 30-23 loss to Seattle, which now seemed light years ahead of Tampa Bay. Huff threw two crushing late interceptions, one in the end zone, and another on first and 10 at the Seahawk 24-yard line with 1:38 to play.

The two-season losing streak was at 19 games.

Mumphord looked like a prophet.

Can't Win for Losing

Trailing 13-0 against Green Bay, Huff was thrown to the Tampa Stadium turf. He writhed in pain and pounded the ground over what would later be diagnosed as a cracked rib. Then Huff heard a loud noise. Could it be? It was.

Fans, reacting to the injury, were cheering.

"I felt like I was going to pass out and I was lying there, and the people are cheering. I'm thinking, "What if I died right here? What would they do then?"" Huff later said.

Tampa Bay's 20th consecutive loss got uglier. Hedberg, Huff's replacement, suffered a concussion. Afterward, he was unable to locate his locker.

Green Bay's only touchdown was set up by a blocked punt. The Packers rushed one man—Jim Gueno—but Bucs punter Dave Green inexplicably took a step to the right and plunked it directly into Gueno's stomach.

Afterward, a despondent McKay used his postgame news conference to apologize to the fans.

McKay's humor returned two weeks later, following a 31-0 loss to the Los Angeles Rams, his first regular-season trip to the L.A. Coliseum.

"Gentlemen, Minnesota lost 27-7 to St. Louis today," McKay said. "Other people have the same problems I have. I just have a longer problem."

Twenty-two consecutive defeats. A longer problem, indeed.

Getting Closer

When the New York Giants came to Tampa, the Bucs' winless plight was profiled by *The New York Times*. "I was part of the group that helped to bring an NFL franchise to Tampa," civic leader Leonard Levy was quoted as saying. "I had nothing to do with the Bucs."

Tampa Bay's offensive ineptitude hit a new low with a 10-0 home loss to the Giants. Five times the Bucs drove inside New York's 20-yard line. Five times the Bucs came away with no points.

"We couldn't score against a strong wind," McKay said.

Case in point: The Bucs had first and goal from the 4-yard line. Ricky Bell, first pick in the 1977 draft, ran four consecutive times—up the middle for no gain, pitch right for no gain, draw play for two yards and pitch right for minus two yards.

Consecutive loss No. 24 came at Detroit, a 16-7 defeat that saw Tampa Bay unable to put it away. With a 7-3 lead in the third quarter—the Bucs had scored first for the initial time in 1977—Jeb Blount hit Isaac Hagins, a 4.4 sprinter, on a crossing pattern that had the makings of a 70-yard touchdown. Alas,

Hagins was run down by aging cornerback Lem Barney, who stripped the ball loose at the Detroit 20-yard line.

It bounded toward the end zone, through the arms of several players before it was recovered (by a Lion, of course) for a touchback. The Lions drove for the go-ahead touchdown.

The following week, McKay jokingly said he considered standing naked on the sidelines at Tampa Stadium. "Maybe that will distract the other quarterback," he said.

It wouldn't have mattered. The Bucs were that bad.

McKay, fully clothed for consecutive loss No. 25, saw his offense again undressed in a 17-0 loss to the Atlanta Falcons. The Bucs had 78 yards of total offense. Heading into the locker room, McKay was doused by a soft drink tossed from overhead. Fans held signs with a popular suggestion: "Throw McKay In The Bay!"

"Our offensive line was horrible," McKay said. "Therefore, our strategy was the same."

Consecutive loss No. 26 came against the Chicago Bears, 10-0, at Tampa Stadium, although Chicago was held scoreless entering the fourth quarter. Chicago's Walter Payton, who earlier in 1977 set the NFL's single-game rushing record with a 275-yard game, labored for his 101 yards on 33 carries. He scored the game's only touchdown.

The Bucs had run the gamut of frustration. But things were about to change.

When the Bucs Come Marching In

Through the first 12 games, the Bucs had scored just four offensive touchdowns. They were on the brink of another winless season. Fans hoped for a miracle. All the Bucs needed was a one-word spark.

Disgrace.

"Everybody got really wide-eyed when they heard that," Lee Roy Selmon said. "Hey, we were a professional team, too. We said, "OK, this has gone on long enough. Let's end this thing.'"

In the locker room at New Orleans, McKay told his players that Saints quarterback Archie Manning said it would be a "disgrace" to lose to the Bucs. To this day, Manning denies making that remark, but admits he told writers that the Saints would be "the laughingstock of the NFL" if they were defeated by Tampa Bay. That simply represented the feeling of every Tampa Bay opponent as the losing streak mounted.

The winless Bucs were frightening in their own way.

Whether McKay fabricated Manning's words, the ploy worked. The Bucs played with purpose. The Saints, who came in 3-9, panicked after falling behind. The Bucs ended their record 26-game losing streak by resoundingly beating the Saints 33-14. They intercepted six New Orleans passes and returned three for touchdowns, tying an NFL record.

"We were strangled by the trauma," said disgraced Saints coach Hank Stram, who burned the game film in front of his team the next day. "We're all ashamed for our people, our fans, our organization."

McKay said he felt the Saints were overlooking the Bucs. Before the game, he noticed Stram and Saints owner John Mecom comparing the quality of their suits. "I had my $2.95 windbreaker on," McKay said.

But McKay brought his solid-gold defense.

From the start, this was a different afternoon for Tampa Bay. The Bucs had two prime opportunities for early touchdowns, but settled for two field goals by Green. Culminating a 71-yard drive, Huff's five-yard pass to Morris Owens made it 13-0, giving the defense a luxury it had rarely enjoyed.

Breathing room.

The Bucs hardly knew how to act when it was over. Linebacker Richard Wood hurried to the locker room because "a grown man ought not to be crying out here in front of all these people." McKay, his voice wavering, choked back tears in an emotional postgame address. He called it "my greatest victory."

"Let this," linebacker Dewey Selmon said, "be the cornerstone."

Tampa Bay's plane ride home, which often resembled a flying casket during the losing streak, became one of the all-time celebrations in team history. Victory cigars were passed around. McKay shook everyone's hand. Massive defensive line coach Abe Gibron danced with the diminutive Hagins.

The party had only begun.

The Frantic Reaction

More than 5,000 fans gathered outside One Buc Place, streaming down West Shore Boulevard, while waiting for the team. Next door, the Swash-buc-lers led cheers from the roof of the Tampa Airport Resort. The Buccaneer Band added new words to an old favorite: "*Oh when the Saints ... go falling down ... Oh when the Saints go falling down ... How I'd like to be in that number ... When the Saints go falling down.*"

The team returned to impassable streets and utter madness.

"I had never seen anything like that, ever," McKay later said. "Not even at USC, when we came back from beating Notre Dame. It's pretty darn hard to lose that many games in a row. It was just our time ... finally."

McKay climbed on top of a car and gave a brief speech to the cheering multitudes. Nearby, somebody waved a handmade sign: "Retrieve McKay From The Bay!"

In the day-after euphoria, McKay was contacted by staffers from NBC-TV's *The Tonight Show*. They wanted him to appear with host Johnny Carson, who had taken several digs at the Bucs

*Coach John McKay is cheered by Tampa fans after the team
returned home from its history-making 33-14 victory at New
Orleans. The victory gave the team its first win and ended an NFL
all-time worst 26-game losing streak. (The Tampa Tribune)*

during monologues from preceding weeks. McKay declined, although the Bucs did send Carson a game football with "Bucs 33, Saints 14" painted on its side.

"I don't need to do it, because I've been on Johnny's show before," McKay said. "I set a ratings record."

McKay also received a classic telegram from an old Hollywood buddy, ageless actor George Burns, star of the movie *Oh, God*.

"Playing God in the movie ... makes me an authority on miracles," Burns's telegram read. "I parted the Red Sea for Moses and won the 1969 World Series for the Mets. Taking care of the Bucs on Sunday was the toughest task of my career. Do me a favor and win No. 2 on your own. Congratulations."

A Winning Streak!

The following week, days before Christmas, the Bucs presented their fans with a gift—another victory.

Prior to a 17-7 win against the St. Louis Cardinals, the Bucs did away with individual introductions. Instead, players ran single file down the middle of the field. They stopped and waved to fans, who stood and cheered.

This time, there was offense. Carter put the Bucs ahead 7-0 with a one-yard run on fourth and goal. How long had it been? On the 372nd offensive play by the 1977 Bucs at Tampa Stadium, they finally had a touchdown at home.

Then they had another—in electrifying fashion. Huff found Owens behind the defense for a picture-perfect 61-yard bomb, caught in stride. After a season of such brutal offensive execution, the play seemed extraordinary.

With the Bucs ahead 14-7 in the third quarter, backed to their 1-yard line, Huff hit Owens again on a 62-yard play. Only

In the final game of the 1977 season, wide receiver Morris Owens scores the Bucs' second home touchdown of the season. The first came minutes earlier from teammate Louis Carter. (The Tampa Tribune)

a shoestring tackle prevented a 99-yard touchdown, but the play set up Green's 24-yard field goal.

At game's end, fans rushed the field and tore down both sets of goal posts. Perhaps never before in NFL history had such optimism surrounded a 2-12 team. But for players and fans, who suffered through practically unprecedented ineptness, it felt so good.

In a cruel irony, McKay's first two NFL victories were against Stram (New Orleans) and Don Coryell (St. Louis), two of his closest friends in coaching. Shortly after losing to Tampa Bay, both coaches were fired.

McKay? Fresh off a 26-game losing streak, he was just getting started.

The (Un)Forgettable Streak

The Bucs lost an NFL record 26 consecutive games during the 1976 and '77 seasons. Fittingly, oddsmakers had the Bucs as underdogs each week.

1976

Date	Result	Spread	Comment
Sept. 12	Oilers 20, Bucs 0	17	So it begins: Bucs manage just 108 yards of total offense
Sept. 19	Chargers 23, Bucs 0	3	Total offense (125 yards) boosted by Parnell Dickinson's 46-yard run
Sept. 26	Bills 14, Bucs 9	10 1/2	Three field goals don't hold up; Bills win in fourth quarter
Oct. 3	Colts 42, Bucs 17	20	Bucs led 3-0, then Colts scored 42 consecutive points
Oct. 10	Bengals 21, Bucs 0	21	Probably could have been much worse
Oct. 17	Seahawks 13, Bucs 10	3	Dave Green's late 35-yard field goal is blocked
Oct. 24	Dolphins 23, Bucs 20	3	Decided by Garo Yepremian's field goal with 55 seconds to play
Oct. 31	Chiefs 28, Bucs 19	6	Chiefs led 20-0 in fourth quarter
Nov. 7	Broncos 48, Bucs 13	11	Broncos score 24 points in fourth quarter
Nov. 14	Jets 34, Bucs 0	7	Aging Joe Namath throws a TD pass
Nov. 21	Browns 24, Bucs 7	15	Browns break 7-7 tie in third quarter
Nov. 28	Raiders 49, Bucs 16	23	Eventual Super Bowl champions roll up 486 yards
Dec. 5	Steelers 42, Bucs 0	26	Bucs manage just 105 yards on 28-degree afternoon
Dec. 12	Patriots 31, Bucs 14	20	Sam Hunt's 68-yard interception return breaks 14-14 tie in third quarter

1977

Date	Result	Spread	Comment
Sept. 18	Eagles 13, Bucs 3	13	Offense goes nowhere with rookie QB Randy Hedberg
Sept. 24	Vikings 9, Bucs 3	14	Fran Tarkenton wins it with third-quarter TD pass on third and 14
Oct. 2	Cowboys 23, Bucs 7	21	Bucs score season's first TD on Richard Wood's fumble return
Oct. 9	Redskins 10, Bucs 0	13	Bucs can't answer Redskins' 10 quick first-quarter points
Oct. 16	Seahawks 30, Bucs 23	1	WR Morris Owens has nine catches, 166 yards in losing cause
Oct. 23	Packers 13, Bucs 0	4 1/2	Packers win despite 218 yards of total offense
Oct. 30	49ers 20, Bucs 10	15	Bucs show some life with a fourth-quarter rally
Nov. 6	Rams 31, Bucs 0	21	Never a chance in McKay's regular-season return to L.A.
Nov. 13	Giants 10, Bucs 0	7	Bucs outgain Giants 287 to 197, but falter in red zone
Nov. 20	Lions 16, Bucs 7	15	Lions blitz Bucs with 13 points in fourth quarter
Nov. 27	Falcons 17, Bucs 0	10	Bucs have 78 yards of offense, four turnovers
Dec. 4	Bears 10, Bucs 0	15	Game was scoreless heading into fourth quarter

Chapter 4

JOHN MCKAY

The Decision

He was the sophisticated, erudite coach at the University of Southern California, a man with four national championships and a darling of the Hollywood set.

One minute, John McKay was a legend, one of college football's untouchables.

The next minute, McKay was presiding over the expansion Bucs, an NFL laughingstock franchise that struggled to make first downs, let alone win games. McKay wore a creamsicle-orange windbreaker and a floppy white golf hat. He twirled his Tampa-made cigars and fired an array of one-liners like a white-haired Groucho Marx.

What happened?

McKay sometimes struggled to explain why he left USC, where he won five Rose Bowls. In candid moments, he admitted he made a mistake, mostly because he underestimated how difficult it would be with an expansion team stocked with has-been and never-was players.

There had been periodic NFL inquiries throughout the years. McKay had turned down the Browns, Patriots and Rams. He also was rumored as a frontrunner for Seattle's expansion franchise.

But he never crossed the line until 1975, when Tampa Bay made its offer. This time, McKay listened.

Bucs owner Hugh Culverhouse stalked McKay, arranging several meetings filled with sweet talk and grand promises. In practical terms, this was McKay's chance to achieve financial security as Culverhouse offered a five-year deal worth between $1.5 to $2 million, an outrageous figure for the mid-1970s. To augment his USC salary, McKay had become a regular on the banquet circuit. Between coaching, recruiting and speaking engagements, he was rarely home.

Most attractive of all, McKay could build from scratch. But he didn't realize all the consequences.

"The way they stocked the teams [through the veteran allocation process] just wasn't a fair way to do it," McKay later said. "People in L.A. thought I was off my rocker to take the Tampa Bay job. I saw the chance to build something that would last. Maybe I was a little naïve. In looking back, I did not know exactly what was entailed in this situation. I don't believe it was conducive to winning."

McKay's deal was essentially agreed upon after the 1975 College All-Star Game in July. Seeking to avoid distractions, he didn't immediately announce his plans, though. That would become a great mistake. Tampa Bay rumors dogged McKay throughout USC's season. With the Trojans at 7-0, McKay finally admitted he was playing out the string.

The Trojans promptly went on a four-game losing streak. Another national championship wouldn't be in the cards, but the Trojans did present a going-away present in the form of a Liberty Bowl victory against previously unbeaten Texas A&M.

Getting to Know You

McKay got off to a rocky start with Tampa Bay fans. And it had little to do with the Bucs' inability to win games.

He was too California cool, somewhat aloof and arrogant. He sparred with Tampa sportscaster Andy Hardy, who hosted McKay's weekly television show. McKay was accustomed to booster-type treatment. Hardy asked pointed questions about why things didn't work. McKay said it felt like an inquisition.

Bucs coach John McKay holds his trademark cigar. (The Tampa Tribune)

Typical exchange:

Hardy: "Coach, if you're running up the middle on first down, and it continually fails to gain yardage, why do you keep calling that play?"

McKay: "Of course, Andy, you wouldn't understand this, but ..."

In later years, McKay said he regretted his perceived image. Making matters worse, McKay refused to give a fake smile or throw a public relations assault at his critics. He didn't care for long telephone conversations, disingenuous glad-handing or social gatherings. He wouldn't change to encourage more love from the fans.

"I've coached this way all my life," McKay once said. "I do not intend to change for this community or any. If I changed, wouldn't that make me a phony? I'm not running for office. And I didn't even ask for this job. I had a job. When I say that, people say I'm arrogant. I'm not. Those are the facts."

Learning How to Win

The Bucs seemed eons away from their 26-game losing streak after beginning 4-4 in 1978, including a 16-10 win at perennial NFC Central Division champion Minnesota, to establish themselves as legitimate postseason threats. Following a 33-19 home win against Chicago, McKay proclaimed, "We are no longer pretenders. We are contenders." Then the momentum halted.

With the opportunity to pass .500 for the first time in franchise history, the Bucs could not protect a late one-point lead at Green Bay. The Packers converted on fourth and 10, positioning themselves for Chester Marcol's 48-yard field goal with 41 seconds remaining and a 9-7 win.

The next week, against the Los Angeles Rams, rookie quarterback Doug Williams suffered a broken jaw after a late above-the-shoulders blow from defensive end Fred Dryer. "There was no penalty called on the play," McKay said. "So Doug must have bit himself in the lip and broke his jaw."

The Bucs gamely rallied behind backup quarterback Mike Rae, but lost 26-23 on Frank Corral's 27-yard field goal with three seconds remaining. Williams would be out until the season's final week. A promising start was wasted, and the Bucs finished 5-11. The larger message: Tampa Bay finally had a foundation. Winning no longer was a novelty.

1979: From Worst to First

"Tampa Bay: Unbeaten, Untied and Unbelievable."

That was the *Sports Illustrated* headline in September 1979. Bucs linebacker Dewey Selmon was on *SI*'s cover, crunching a running back from the Rams. Tampa Bay was headed to a 5-0 start, an eventual NFC Central Division title and a serious run at Super Bowl XIV.

The Bucs, not even two seasons removed from their 0-26 beginning, were the toast of the NFL.

"We had the makings of a team that could compete," McKay said. "I didn't think it was a world championship team [before the season]. But we had a lot of very good ingredients."

Namely, the NFL's No. 1-ranked defense, paced by Lee Roy Selmon, the league's defensive player of the year; a revitalized running game, led by Ricky Bell, who rushed for 1,263 yards, and rookie Jerry Eckwood; the retooled offensive line, which included rookie Greg Roberts and converted defensive lineman Charley Hannah on the right side; and Williams, who came into his own, even with a dismal 41.8 completion percentage.

"We only gave up 12 sacks all year [after allowing 52 in 1978], but that was mostly due to Doug," Hannah said. "He'd throw it away and hurt his individual statistics, but he'd help the team."

"It's simple math—I'd rather be second and 10 instead of second and 16," Williams said. "I didn't care about my stats. When we played the Rams, I saw Pat Haden complete three straight passes. Well, that made it fourth and 2. That's not winning football. We were interested in winning. That's what the '79 Bucs were all about."

The Playoff Run

Coming off a 31-3 win against the New York Giants, the Bucs were 9-3 and one victory away from the franchise's first division title and playoff berth. When the Vikings visited Tampa Stadium, team officials made certain to grease the goalposts, discouraging fans from trying to rip them down.

But this wouldn't be a day to celebrate.

The Vikings blocked three kicks and a punt, dazing the Bucs. Williams scored the apparent tying touchdown when he cartwheeled into the end zone on a 13-yard scramble with 19 seconds remaining. Then Neil O'Donoghue's point-after kick was blocked by Minnesota's Wally Hilgenberg, preserving the Vikings' 23-22 win.

A one-week setback became a two-week slump when the Bucs lost 14-0 at home to Chicago, despite limiting the Bears to 164 yards. The bottom fell out completely with a 23-7 road loss to the San Francisco 49ers, who came in at 1-13.

The Bucs, once the clear NFC frontrunner, had a three-game losing streak (with 17 turnovers) and were in danger of missing the playoffs. Linebacker David Lewis suggested the

Bucs were choking. *Tampa Tribune* sports editor Tom McEwen took it one step further, rechristening the team as "Chokeneers."

An infuriated McKay said "people who use the [choke] terms are no better than snakes." He predicted victory in the regular-season finale against Kansas City before adding, "What am I going to do? Predict a defeat?"

In keeping with the late-season trend, nothing came easy. A torrential downpour transformed Tampa Stadium's normally redoubtable turf into a quagmire. Tampa Bay's defense was sensational, allowing the Chiefs just 80 yards, but the offense couldn't convert opportunities into points.

O'Donoghue produced the game's only points in the fourth quarter, a 19-yard field goal that was made possible by Tom Blanchard, who quickly steadied a low snap.

The Bucs had an unartistic 3-0 victory. Nobody really lamented the lack of style points. In only the franchise's fourth season, the Bucs were going to the playoffs.

McKay's Finest Hour

On the *NFL Today* set at Tampa Stadium, CBS-TV announcer Brent Musburger made this pregame proclamation: "I just hope Tampa Bay can keep it close for a while."

Expectations, to say the least, were minimal for the opening-round NFC playoff game against the Eagles. Even though the Bucs were at home, they had stumbled into the postseason. McKay stayed with Williams at quarterback, despite 11 interceptions in the final three games, and some viewed that as blind faith.

Tampa Bay's doubters quickly lost ammunition. Williams played under control. The Bucs went 80 yards in 18 plays on the opening drive, which took 9:25 off the clock. Bell scored on a

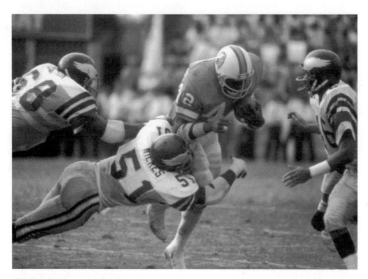

Ricky Bell rushed for 142 yards in the 1979 playoff win against Philadelphia, thought of by many as Coach McKay's finest hour. (The Tampa Tribune)

four-yard run on fourth down, setting a hard-edged tone for an afternoon that produced a 24-17 victory.

"Once again, it was us against the world," Lewis said. "The more people who said we were a fluke, the madder and more determined we got."

"We weren't a bunch of great individual football players," Wood said. "But we were a great, great football team."

That was evident against the Eagles. Strong safety Mark Cotney played close to the line, jamming six-foot-eight Eagles receiver Harold Carmichael. Philadelphia running back Wilbert Montgomery was shadowed all afternoon and ran for only 35 yards.

It was a coming-out party for the team and its orange-clad legions of fans. "That crowd was the damnedest thing I've ever seen," Eagles defensive lineman Claude Humphrey said.

Suddenly, everything broke in favor of the Bucs. When the Rams upset Dallas in the other NFC semifinal, the Bucs learned they would host the NFC Championship Game. The opponent: A Rams team they had dominated, 21-6, back in September. A trip to Super Bowl XIV, at Pasadena's Rose Bowl, was there for the taking. All the Bucs needed was one more victory.

One Game Short

All the Rams saw was a sea of orange, crackling like a brush fire. On cue, the 72,033 fans at Tampa Stadium, who had partied all afternoon, serenaded the nation with the Bucs' unofficial fight song.

> *Hey, hey, Tampa Bay,*
> *The Bucs know how to shine,*
> *Hey, hey, Tampa Bay,*
> *The Bucs know how to shine,*
> *If we're in trouble, that's OK,*
> *We can pull it out,*
> *Because we know we're on the top,*
> *When we stand up,*
> *STAND UP AND SHOUT!*

Rich Saul, a 10th-year center for the Rams, had one conclusion amid the deafening din: "This place is insane."

Anyone who predicted a Bucs-Rams matchup in the NFC Championship Game could have pleaded insanity, too. But this was a day for long shots. It was January 6, 1980, a cool, crisp early evening in Tampa. The Rams, perceived as underachievers, had lost four of the previous five NFC Championship Games. The Bucs were a popular pick.

"When Super Bowl Sunday arrives 15 days from now, the Pittsburgh Steelers and—yes!—the Tampa Bay Buccaneers will trot onto the turf in Pasadena, California," wrote The Associated Press.

"My gosh, we could taste it," Wood said. "We were in our house. We were supremely confident. The Super Bowl. It was right there for us. But you know what? You're not promised anything in this game."

The Rams controlled the clock. The Bucs' conservative game plan went nowhere. By the fourth quarter, Tampa Bay's two best players, Williams and Lee Roy Selmon, were sidelined by injuries.

The Rams managed three short field goals by Corral, winning 9-0. It remains the only NFL championship game without a touchdown. Tampa Bay seemingly scored on a late TD pass from Rae to tight end Jimmie Giles, but it was negated by an illegal motion penalty.

Some thought it had all the excitement of a root canal. But the players remember a game fraught with tension, a physical contest that became a thinking-man's street fight. Its symbol was Rams defensive end Jack Youngblood, who played with a broken leg.

"People say, 'Well, you had a great season, you came farther than anyone expected,'" McKay said. "People don't understand. In a game like that, there's the exhilaration of winning and the absolute devastation of losing. You only get so many chances. You had better take advantage of them."

1980: An Unhappy Aftermath

Despite opening with two victories, including a nationally televised 10-9 rematch win against the Rams, the 1980 Bucs regressed to 5-10-1. The top-ranked defense dropped to No. 20 in the NFL, once wasting a 486-yard passing performance by Williams in a 38-30 loss at Minnesota.

In the final month, while still in the playoff hunt, the Bucs three times staked a 10-0 lead in the first half. They lost each game.

Even on positive plays, things seemed out of synch. Against Green Bay, Wood returned an interception 55 yards for a tying touchdown. Fired up by the pivotal play, Wood turned in the end zone to celebrate with his teammates. But no one was within 30 yards of him. He was alone.

"All the emotion we once had, it wasn't there anymore," Wood said. "Like we were just, I don't know, flat."

Several years later, team officials revealed the team had a drug problem.

"I wanted to cry out," Culverhouse said. "I was angry. I was upset and hurt. It was Party Time, U.S.A."

"There's no question we had a drug problem," McKay said. "There were some fine players who made some mistakes. I did what I could to get rid of those players. We came back (in later seasons), but I never realized how serious the drugs were."

1981: Return to the Playoffs

The 1981 Bucs seemed headed for another disappointing season. They stood at 5-6 following a 24-7 home loss to Denver. McKay sensed things slipping away. That's when he brought quarterbacks coach Bill Nelsen down from the press box to the field, so play-calling could be better coordinated. That's when he shortened practices. And that's when the Bucs began to win again.

They ran off three consecutive victories, including a 24-23 win against the Atlanta Falcons. Williams's 71-yard TD pass to Kevin House put the Bucs ahead to stay, but it wasn't preserved until Scott Hutchinson deflected a 45-yard field-goal attempt by Atlanta's Mick Luckhurst on the final play.

The Bucs, with an opportunity to win the NFC Central title at home, fell to San Diego 24-23 in the final minute. That left one game. Tampa Bay (8-7) vs. Detroit (8-7) at the Pontiac Silverdome, where the Lions were unbeaten under quarterback Eric Hipple. Winner got the division crown and a playoff berth. Loser stayed home.

"Nobody thought we could win up there," Williams said. "Nobody except us."

Detroit fans were in a festive mood, perhaps spurred on by this suggestion from a *Detroit News* columnist: "Let It Ripple With Hipple."

The Bucs took control when Brown intercepted Hipple in the end zone and returned it to the 16-yard line. Williams promptly hit House with an 84-yard TD pass, sending a clear message that Tampa Bay was primed for the upset.

By the time nose tackle David Logan scored on a 21-yard fumble return, after Selmon leveled Hipple in the fourth quarter, the Bucs were on their way to a 20-17 victory.

"They had the champagne on ice over in their locker room," McKay told his players afterward. "But we'll just stay here and drink our beer."

The celebration would not last long. The playoffs brought a sobering 38-0 loss at Dallas. Williams, the most difficult quarterback to sack over three seasons, was dropped four times and twice called for intentional grounding. He also had four interceptions.

1982: Striking Back

The playoffs seemed just a faint hope following the 57-day strike by NFL players in 1982. The Bucs lost their first two games before the work stoppage, then were defeated at Dallas when play resumed. An expanded playoff format, the so-called Super Bowl Tournament, made for an easier path, but the Bucs showed no signs of improvement.

Then the Bucs won five of their last six games behind Williams. First, trailing 21-6 in the third quarter, he engineered a rally against Detroit to win 23-21. In a do-or-die regular-season finale against Chicago, the Bucs trailed 23-6 with seven minutes remaining in the third quarter. Williams threw an interception returned for a touchdown and lost a key fumble.

But he finished 25 of 49 for 367 yards (his second highest passing total) and positioned Bill Capece for his game-tying 40-yard field goal late in regulation play. The greatest comeback in team history was assured in overtime when James Wilder burst for a 47-yard run, setting up Capece's 33-yard game-winner to beat Chicago 26-23.

The Bucs again drew a trip to Dallas for the playoffs. This time, it was much more competitive. The Bucs actually led 17-16 in the fourth quarter, but had a first down negated by a holding penalty. On the next play, Williams's pass was intercepted by Monty Hunter, who returned it 19 yards for a score. Dallas won 30-17. After solid play down the stretch, the Bucs were finished.

Nobody knew it yet, but so were Williams's days in Tampa.

Losing Doug Williams

The selection of Williams in 1978 was a daring move; a black quarterback playing in the South.

McKay never blinked.

"I'm 55 years old," McKay said. "If Doug Williams isn't the future, we'll have to start over, and I'm too tired to start over."

McKay's heart was about to be ripped out. Following the 1982 season, Williams bolted for the United States Football League following a bitter contract dispute. He was full of spite and wished the worst for his former franchise. "I hope they go 0 and 16," he said.

Bucs coach John McKay and quarterback Doug Williams walk off the field together for the final time following a 30-17 playoff defeat at Dallas that closed Tampa Bay's 1982 season. (The Tampa Tribune)

The Bucs nearly obliged. With the offense in free fall, the Bucs lost their first nine games in 1983. The lowlight was a meeting between the 1-11 Bucs and 1-11 Houston Oilers. It was dubbed Repus Bowl I (Repus is Super spelled backward) by *The Tampa Tribune*.

For fans, it was open season on McKay. A coin dealer took out an ad in *The St. Petersburg Times*, offering McKay $1,200 in silver dollars if he tried any of several suggested plays (including a double-reverse fake flea-flicker). Meanwhile, an ad in *The Clearwater Sun* presented McKay with a free membership to a golf club. The catch: Membership was for Sunday afternoons only.

Without Williams as the catalyst, some veteran players grew insecure about their fate. McKay felt powerless and disillusioned at the loss of his player. "It was a terrible, terrible mistake," McKay later said.

The Bucs, 2-14 in 1983, looked rudderless. The postseason run was over. Soon, McKay would experience the beginning of the end.

Giving Up

McKay hinted at retirement in an interview with *The Lakeland Ledger* before the 1984 season, suggesting that he couldn't endure another dreadful year. The outlook seemed promising, though, when quarterback Steve DeBerg replaced Jack Thompson in the lineup and engineered a 3-3 start. Then the bottom dropped out with a four-game losing streak.

Before the season, McKay wanted to obtain place-kicker Jan Stenerud, a future Hall of Famer who could shore up a trouble-some position. Culverhouse nixed the deal. "We were being too cheap," McKay later recounted.

The Bucs' fourth consecutive loss sapped McKay's spirit. After rallying to tie the Vikings at 24-24 in the final minute, the game seemed destined for overtime. But on fourth and nine, after an incomplete pass with 20 seconds remaining, the Bucs were called for pass interference. Minnesota's kicker was summoned for a long field goal attempt.

Stenerud was good from 53 yards on the game's final play.

As he walked off the field, McKay muttered under his breath, "I don't need this."

The following day, McKay announced his resignation, effective at season's end.

The Final Day

McKay, with lame-duck status, went 3-3 in his final games with the Bucs. Playoff opportunities were long gone, but the games were eventful. Especially the finale, a 41-21 win against the New York Jets. An otherwise sharp performance by Tampa Bay was overshadowed by a failed attempt to set an NFL record for running back James Wilder.

Wilder was in reach of the single-season record for total yards from scrimmage. After scoring on a four-yard touchdown run, making it 41-14 with 1:21 to play, Wilder needed 16 more yards. The Bucs three times attempted an onside kick, in an obvious attempt for last-ditch yards by Wilder, but after two penalties, the last kick was recovered by the Jets.

McKay's retort? He ordered the defense to allow a New York touchdown.

The Jets scored in four plays against a Tampa Bay defense that essentially laid down. The Bucs offered no resistance— some players even backpedaled—on Johnny Hector's two-yard TD run.

The Jets then tried an onside kick of their own, but it was recovered by the Bucs. With the game reduced to a Keystone Kops-like grudge match, the seething Jets, keying on Wilder, held him to zero yards on three more late-game touches.

Wilder ended with 2,229 total yards from scrimmage, which was No. 3 (at the time) in NFL history.

"The way it ended was a total embarrassment by the NFL," Jets coach Joe Walton said. "It set it back 20 years. It was completely uncalled for."

Several Jets players approached McKay afterward and screamed obscenities. McKay was unapologetic. "It embarrassed me to hear language like that on the football field," he said, smirking.

New York media referred to the coach as "McGutless." The integrity-minded NFL was not amused by the late-game proceedings. More than two months later, McKay received the largest fine ever assessed against an NFL coach, nearly $10,000, according to news reports. Culverhouse paid the fine.

"I'm sorry about the furor, but what could I do?" McKay later said. "Somebody was sure to walk away angry, the Jets or our players and Tampa fans. If I had a choice, I'd rather make them mad in New York than here in the town where I live and work."

At the Pro Bowl, Wilder's quotes were revealing: "I didn't like it at all. If I have to set a record that way, I don't want it."

The controversy never subsided. As for McKay, to the end, he did it his way. "We play them again next year and the only problem is McKay won't be there," Jets quarterback Ken O'Brien said in the bitter locker room.

That didn't seem to matter. The final from 1985's rematch: Jets 62, Bucs 28.

Life After the Bucs

Just before completing the 1985 season as team president, McKay resigned. Now completely out of football for the first time in his adult life, McKay stayed far away from the Bucs. He was inducted into the College Football Hall of Fame in 1988, and ventured back to Tampa Stadium when inducted into the team's Krewe of Honor to a loud ovation. Otherwise, he was rarely spotted in public, unless it was with a small gathering of friends or on the golf course. Why the low profile?

"Those people out there might kill me," he said in 1989. "You know I'm still getting blamed for what's going on with that team, and I haven't coached there in five years."

It was different when McKay's son, Rich, joined the Tampa Bay front office (against the old coach's wishes). Rich McKay soon was elevated to general manager, where he oversaw the franchise's renaissance. McKay attended many games and watched from a private box. He was excited about the team's turnaround, and became a semi-regular at practices and training camp.

The Bucs were on the verge of a world championship. Unfortunately, McKay wouldn't live to see that day.

McKay's health wasn't good in his final years. He underwent quadruple-bypass heart surgery in 1996. In May 2001, he was admitted to St. Joseph's Hospital with complications from diabetes. Nearly one month later—on June 10, 2001—he died of kidney failure.

Win One for the Quipper

In McKay's early days as a head coach, he vowed to avoid clichés and dry analysis after games. "None of that stuff like having our backs against the wall or that other junk every coach since Amos Alonzo Stagg has used," he said.

He could be searingly sarcastic, wry, flippant and downright hilarious.

Here's a sampling of McKay's famous quips, often repeated, but never duplicated:

After a 51-0 loss to Notre Dame: "I told our players there were 700 million Chinese who didn't even know the game was played. The next week, I got five letters from China saying, "What happened, Coach?""

On matching up against the opposing coach: "When the game starts, there are two idiots. When the game ends, there's only one. The idea is to make sure that idiot is not you."

Told that place-kicker Pete Rajecki said he became nervous when McKay watched him kick: "Please inform Mr. Rajecki that I plan to attend all games."

On what he thought of his team's execution: "I'm in favor of it."

Asked where he stood on an upcoming game at Pittsburgh: "With Custer."

On whether a potential blizzard at Pittsburgh could slow down the Steelers: "It probably would snow only on our side of the field."

On facing Joe Namath during a 34-0 loss to the Jets in 1976: "Our guys were nice to him. When they knocked him down, they helped him to his feet. That was gentlemanly. I thought one stood around long enough to get his autograph."

On punter/kicker Dave Green, who was slumping in 1977: "He has become our catch-all player. He's catching all kind of hell."

On ending the franchise's 26-game losing streak by beating New Orleans: "Three or four plane crashes and we're in the playoffs."

On his first season in Tampa Bay, as it approached 0-14: "I'm so embarrassed, I've taken to wearing a disguise. I've got a fake beard, fake nose, fake hat, but people still keep stopping me on the street, asking for my autograph. Now they think I am Abe Lincoln."

After being told his teams didn't play with emotion: "Emotion is overrated. My wife is very emotional. She can't play worth a damn."

On a goal-line fumble by Bell, when two Bucs were close enough to recover the ball, but celebrated prematurely: "They were too busy officiating. They were standing there with their hands raised, like an Italian during World War II."

On an improved kicking game: "Our kicking game was second to none. We made every one. By next week, we might be third to none."

On going to a shotgun offense, grudgingly, after several seasons of being criticized for ignoring that option: "Tonight, we unveiled our team shotgun or spread, which was used by Amos Alonzo Stagg in 1902."

On an interception, returned for a touchdown by rookie linebacker Jeff Davis during a 1982 exhibition game: "He scored the first time he ever touched the ball. That's quite a feat. It was last accomplished, I believe, by Red Grange."

On Capece's 27-yard field goal with 25 seconds to play, which clinched a 23-21 win against Detroit to preserve Tampa Bay's playoff hopes in 1982: "Capece's kick? No, I've never seen anything that gutty. Oh, once in World War II, I saw a guy pull nine people out of an airplane. Besides that, it was the most courageous thing I've seen."

On sports writers: "I said on my TV show they didn't know a quarterback from a banana stand, and someone sent me a crate of bananas. This week, I'm going to say most sports writers don't know a quarterback from a Mercedes."

On an injury-plagued season: "We've had too many injuries to be a consistent winner in the NFL. If we had a normal string of injuries and this [poor] record, I would shoot myself to the moon and not come back."

On whether his 1984 midseason resignation announcement, which immediately preceded a 20-17 win against the playoff-bound New York Giants, sent the team into disarray: "I hope they were disarrayed. We won. We have been in array plenty of times this season, and we lost."

Chapter 5

LEE ROY SELMON, HALL OF FAMER

The year was 1977 and the Bucs were locked in a scoreless tie with the Chicago Bears at halftime. Inside the visitors' locker room, an assistant coach approached Bears offensive tackle Ted Albrecht with some encouraging words.

Albrecht raised his head to reveal the face of a beaten man. "Coach," Albrecht said, "there are four things in this world I do not want to do under any circumstance. No. 1, I don't want to milk a cobra. No. 2, I don't want to be buried at sea. No. 3, I don't want to be hit in the head with a hockey puck. And No. 4, I don't want to play the second half against Lee Roy Selmon."

The Right Decision

Plenty went wrong for the Bucs when they entered the NFL in 1976. But one thing went perfectly right: Selecting Selmon, a defensive end from Oklahoma, to lead off the draft.

Speculation had the Bucs considering Selmon, Arizona State cornerback Mike Haynes and California running back Chuck Muncie. The debate didn't last long, although Ron Wolf, then the Bucs' vice president of football operations, looked hard at Haynes.

"Lee Roy was the best player, no question," Wolf said. "It came down to the fact that you could take Mike Haynes out of the game, but you couldn't take Lee Roy out of the game."

Selmon was a consensus first-team All-American. He won the Outland Trophy and the Lombardi Award. But the Sooners were on probation and banned from television appearances in 1974 and '75, so Selmon's exploits weren't widely seen. Oklahoma coach Barry Switzer called it "the most unwatched great team in college football history."

The Bucs had seen enough. When Wolf and Bucs owner Hugh Culverhouse traveled to Norman, Oklahoma, for a meeting with Selmon and Switzer, it became a formality.

Coach John McKay, Lee Roy Selmon, and vice president of football operations Ron Wolf on the day the Bucs selected Selmon with the first pick in the 1976 draft. (The Tampa Tribune)

By the time Selmon's career finished prematurely in 1986, after he was diagnosed with a herniated disc in his back, he had a franchise-record 78 1/2 sacks, six Pro Bowl selections and one NFL Defensive Player of the Year honor. His No. 63 jersey was retired. In 1995, he became the franchise's only player elected to the Pro Football Hall of Fame. Later, the city of Tampa named an expressway in Selmon's honor.

"We knew we drafted a great player," former Bucs coach John McKay once said. "Then we began learning what a great person we had drafted."

Back Home in Oklahoma

The Selmon story began in tiny Eufaula, Oklahoma, where he was the youngest of nine children. His father, Lucious Sr., was a sharecropper and the family lived in a white-framed home of approximately 650 square feet. It had no indoor plumbing, no refrigerator, no air conditioner.

The family couldn't afford a tractor. The Selmon boys pushed a plow behind mules on the 160 acres of rented land. They baled hay, tended 150-pound hogs and milked cows. Even as they grew into 230-pound teenagers, Lee Roy still shared a bed with his older brother, Dewey.

"To others, it probably looked like we had nothing," Lee Roy said. "But in reality, we had everything."

Everything meant having enough money for survival and the church collection plate, and enough love and support from a family that thrived on its togetherness. Soon, that family became best known for football.

Lucious Jr., Dewey and Lee Roy played for the Eufaula High Ironheads, transforming the state's smallest Class 2A team into a powerhouse. Lee Roy was chubby at first. His football pants kept falling down. His shoes didn't fit. After only one practice, he wanted to quit. But he listened to his mother, Jessie, who told him to keep trying.

Eventually, the Selmon brothers became a trio of fearsome All-America defensive linemen at OU. Bumper stickers and posters were seen around the state: "God Bless Mrs. Selmon." As for Mrs. Selmon, she thanked her God for this: Each of the brothers graduated from Oklahoma with honors.

Brotherly Love

Selmon was honored to become Tampa Bay's No. 1 overall selection. But later in the day, he received more good news. The Bucs took Dewey in the second round.

"We had always played together," Selmon said. "It was said that was going to stop. Now, all of a sudden, we were together again. Words can't describe how good I felt."

Lee Roy and Dewey were inseparable in many ways. In fact, Dewey once asked Lee Roy to Eufaula High's senior prom.

"It was a small class and we didn't have anyone else to go with," Dewey said with a laugh. "Maybe we were kind of shy, too. There were girls to dance with once we got there, but I guess you could pretty much say we did everything together."

Yet, they were opposite personalities. As a coach once said, "Lee Roy will tackle the running back, then help him up. Dewey will tackle him … then step on him!"

Mr. Nice Guy

For someone who inspired fear in opponents, Selmon's off-field personality was disarming. He was quiet. Nice. Gentle.

True story: Selmon's name was misspelled as "Leroy" all the way through his rookie season in Tampa Bay. In first grade, Selmon's teacher told him no one had a two-word name like Lee Roy. It was "Leroy." Selmon complied because, as he recounted later, his mother told him he shouldn't ever correct his teacher.

When a Tampa reporter learned of the discrepancy, he asked Selmon about his preference. Selmon said he wanted Lee Roy, "the way my mother gave it to me," but quickly added, "if it's all right with everybody else."

Another true story: At Oklahoma, Selmon's future wife, Claybra, was leery about their first date. "The football players on campus were so used to girls falling all over them," she said. "I had a preconceived notion that all football players would be like that."

After a black-tie affair at the Oklahoma governor's mansion in 1975, Selmon walked Claybra to her front door. There was an awkward moment of silence. Their eyes met. Then Selmon offered a good-night handshake.

On the field it was more of the same. Bucs quarterback Doug Williams, after taking a pounding, used to get angry. Selmon had chances to level the opposing quarterback when no one was watching, but usually opted to just push him over.

"I remember saying, 'Lee Roy, why don't you clobber that guy?'" Williams said. "He'd always give me that shrug and just say, 'Come on, guy.'"

Nobody could make Selmon mad. Once at Dallas, Selmon was grabbed by the legs and literally tackled by his blocker. The official did nothing. Selmon popped up and vented his rage: "Heck! Heck! Dang! Dang!"

He was chop-blocked in Minnesota and carried off the field. Teammates fumed and bowed up for retribution. Selmon, still dazed, softly asked a teammate, "They're cheating. Why are they doing that?"

Cornerstone of the Defense

Selmon quickly became an NFL star. But playing in the smaller market of Tampa, for a team that began 0-26, didn't help his national exposure.

"Without question, Lee Roy was the best defensive end I ever played against," former Bears offensive tackle Jimbo Covert said in 1995. "If Lee Roy would've played in a city like Chicago or New York, he would've had even more name recognition. And if you compare him with most defensive ends out there today, well, there is no comparison."

Selmon's early exploits were overshadowed by the franchise's winless plight. In 1977, when the Bucs went 2-12, they would have finished at .500 had the offense simply averaged two touchdowns per game. The defense ranked 13th in the NFL. Selmon had 13 sacks in his second season (in a 14-game schedule), including three in the franchise's first victory.

Never was there a sense that Selmon was disgusted participating in so many lost causes.

"Lee Roy just said, 'No matter who I play, I'm going to play well,'" Dewey Selmon said. "If Lee Roy had said just once, 'This really stinks,' it would have sent negative vibrations through the whole team, and they'd still have been trying for that first winning season. But the best player said, 'Let's go play,' and we went and played."

During the good times, Selmon elevated his play to higher levels. In the 1979 opener, Selmon picked up a fumble caused by Wally Chambers and raced in for a 29-yard touchdown against Detroit, his first score since playing for the Eufaula. In the franchise's first playoff game, Selmon had back-to-back sacks of Ron Jaworski to end the third quarter, quelling an Eagle rally.

"At that point, I was starting to think about retiring," said Eagles offensive tackle Stan Walters, who drew Selmon that day. "Lee Roy got the best of me. As I look back, I can honestly say Lee Roy helped me see the light at the end of the tunnel."

Some still wonder what Selmon would have been like had he been turned loose as a pass rusher. The Bucs stressed a "bend, but don't break" philosophy and emphasized playing the run. Selmon's technical excellence didn't show up on the stat sheet, but it was noticed by teammates and opponents.

Said former Lions quarterback Gary Danielson: "If he played in a major market, especially in today's game where more pass rushing is stressed, there's no doubt in my mind that everybody would be talking about a player being the 'next Lee Roy Selmon' and not the 'next Lawrence Taylor.'"

"Nobody could handle Lee Roy one on one," Williams said. "It's too bad he played in a three-man front. If he had been in a four-man front, they would've banned Lee Roy from the game."

An Early Retirement

Selmon was in his prime when he played in the 1985 Pro Bowl, making his sixth trip to Hawaii. But at the game, a herniated disk was discovered in his back. It required surgery and forced him to miss the entire 1985 season, Tampa Bay's first under Coach Leeman Bennett.

The Bucs wobbled to 2-14 and sunk to the 26th-rated defense in the NFL. Selmon's return was supposed to help matters.

Bucs defensive end Lee Roy Selmon, in his final game with Tampa Bay, sacks New York Jets quarterback Ken O'Brien in 1984. (The Tampa Tribune)

But he never came back.

At age 31, after only nine NFL seasons, Selmon retired. At the formal announcement on April 23, 1986, Culverhouse proclaimed, "There will never be another 63." He meant it literally, too. The Bucs announced plans to retire Selmon's No. 63 jersey.

"I pretty much let it go quickly," said Selmon, who became a full-time banker and later athletic director at the University of South Florida. "From the standpoint of my health, it was the right decision. It was a matter of listening to my body. I didn't want to leave the game not being able to walk."

The shortened career seemingly jeopardized his chances for induction into the Pro Football Hall of Fame. But a distinct impression had been made.

Voting for the Hall of Fame

Selmon was bypassed during his first four chances to become a finalist for Pro Football Hall of Fame consideration. Then came the Class of 1995.

From an original list of 58 nominees, the 34-man selection board received a list of 15 finalists. Selmon finally made the cut.

On January 28, 1995, the day before Super Bowl XXIX in Miami, the selection board gathered to elect another class. Longtime *Tampa Tribune* sports editor and columnist Tom McEwen, who had joined the board in 1976, spoke on Selmon's behalf.

The night before an early morning meeting, McEwen was nervous and unable to sleep. He changed his notes a few times. His emphasis: Don't brow beat the selectors. Describe how Selmon helped a woeful expansion team mature into a playoff contender. Use some humor.

McEwen's final remarks: "The only two things Lee Roy Selmon has not achieved in life, as I see it, are salvation and the Pro Football Hall of Fame. I am certain the Good Lord will see that he'll achieve salvation, but only you and I can put him in the Hall of Fame. I believe he deserves it. I know he will do it honor. Thank you."

Selmon made the final 10, then the final six (along with Dan Dierdorf, Jim Finks, Steve Largent, Dwight Stephenson and Kellen Winslow). Selmon needed 26 votes out of 33 (one selector was absent) to make the Hall of Fame. The final vote was secret.

Pete Elliott, who supervised the selection process, announced the new Hall of Famers in alphabetical order: Finks, Jordan, Largent, Selmon and Winslow.

McEwen kept his cool, but grinned broadly and shook hands with other writers from his newspaper.

"I didn't get Lee Roy in the Hall of Fame," McEwen said. "But I didn't louse up and keep him out either."

The Weekend in Canton

Selmon chose his brother, Dewey, as his presenter during induction ceremonies on July 29, 1995. Dewey Selmon said, "I really hope that when all the kids who dream about playing this game that would walk through and see the representations of these athletes, they would look on Lee Roy Selmon and say, 'Yeah, one day, I dream of playing the game like Lee Roy.' Further than that, 'I want to be the person that Lee Roy Selmon represents.'"

Selmon's induction speech gave credit to his parents, siblings, wife and children. "It's not me going into the Hall of Fame," he said. "It's we, us. That's how it has always been with the Selmon family, and how it always will be." Thirty-three members of Selmon's family were present.

He spoke of Culverhouse and McKay, his teammates, the Tampa Bay fans. He praised his coaches, particularly McKay and Abe Gibron, the defensive line coach.

"Lee Roy was almost unblockable," said McKay. "At a time when we were pretty fair, he was what made us pretty fair. I don't think the Hall of Fame is complete without him."

The Quarterbacks Talk Back

A sampling of thoughts from former NFL quarterbacks who were sacked by Selmon:

Terry Bradshaw, Steelers: "In our best years, Tampa Bay wasn't all that good. But Lee Roy Selmon was the one guy on that team that scared us. You had to double-team him because he'd kill you otherwise."

Lynn Dickey, Packers: "Lee Roy played hard every play. He never took a down off. And you couldn't tell if he was being paid 100 bucks a game or a million bucks a game. It didn't matter. He went all out all the time."

Steve Fuller, Chiefs: "My vision of Lee Roy is the same as most quarterbacks in the league. With me on my back and looking up at Lee Roy with the sunshine behind his head."

David Whitehurst, Packers: "The best defensive lineman I've ever seen. Period. He'd make the play, turn around and line up again. That's how the game is meant to be played."

Bert Jones, Colts: "I know this sounds crazy, but you enjoy playing against people of that caliber. As disenchanting as it was every time he hit you, he was such an even-tempered kind of guy. It was as if he was apologizing to you for beating your brains out."

Phil Simms, Giants: "When we looked at the tapes, it was amazing what Lee Roy Selmon was doing in our backfield. It was a good thing I was young and determined at that time or I might not have survived that game. In all honesty, it was the only game I ever played in the NFL where I felt like other quarterbacks felt going against our own Lawrence Taylor. Someone who came in and hit with such speed and force."

The (Would-Be) Blockers Speak Out

A sampling of reactions from former NFL players who tried to block Selmon.

Ron Singleton, 49ers: "When I watched him on film against Minnesota, Rickey Young cut (blocked) him, but Lee Roy just flipped in the air and kept on running. Bobb McKittrick, our offensive line coach, said, 'Was that a man or was that a cat?' The first time I played him, I think I lost 15 pounds in the first half. My wrists were actually hurting from hitting his chest."

Bubba Paris, 49ers: "When I was a rookie, they told me Lee Roy Selmon was an automatic choice for the Pro Bowl. I just said, 'I'm not voting for him. I've never played against him. He can't be that good.' Then I played him. There were plays I never even touched him. It was a major accomplishment just to get my hands on him."

Ted Petersen, Steelers: "I remember one play where he took one of his powerful arms and knocked the offensive lineman to the ground with a club move. With the other arm, he knocked the blocking fullback to the ground and then he made a form tackle on the ball carrier. We were all just amazed."

Jon Kolb, Steelers: "I had a rookie guard, Craig Wolfley, playing next to me and we weren't communicating real well yet. Lee Roy blows past me before I can even move. I fall down trying to get a hand, a leg, an arm—whatever—on him. I'm laying on the ground and all I'm thinking is, "I killed (Steelers quarterback) Terry Bradshaw because I couldn't block Lee Roy. Oh my God, Bradshaw is dead.'"

Chris Dieterich, Lions: "It's like a film strip that breaks. Where it's spliced together there's a couple of scenes that are missing and—blip—it's skipped ahead. That's what it looks like from behind your face mask to go against Lee Roy Selmon. All of a sudden, your eyeballs roll back in your head and he's past you."

Irv Pankey, Rams: "He was a sportsman. No dances, no fingers pointing. I don't know how many Lee Roys are left. The game has changed so much, and so have the bank accounts. They're bigger, and so are the egos. When I think of Lee Roy, I think of how different the game is."

Chapter 6

THE LOST YEARS

A New Era—Or Error?

In 1985, the Bucs entered a new era.

An era without Lee Roy Selmon.

An era without John McKay's wisecracks.

An era when fans wondered if the banished Doug Williams had placed a curse upon the franchise.

An era when the Bucs became the butts of many jokes throughout the sports world. It was worse than expansion, worse than 0 and 26. At least then, there was an excuse. The franchise was just beginning. The players were young. The future held promise, and that promise was realized, if only for a while.

But this? It never seemed to end.

This wasn't Go For 0. It was Go For Bo.

Not surprisingly, Bo (Jackson) said no.

From 1985-95, Tampa Bay's head coaches were Leeman Bennett, Ray Perkins, Richard Williamson and Sam Wyche. During that inglorious era, the Bucs played 176 games.

They lost 125 of them.

It was the guts of an era that produced 14 consecutive losing seasons, all but one of them with double-digit defeat totals.

The Season Unravels

Culverhouse hired Bennett, the former Falcons' coach who had been out of football selling RVs, to replace McKay. But Bennett's Bucs began 0-9; opponents scored 30 points or more in six of those games.

In the locker room, there was much grumbling about the scheme of new defensive coordinator Doug Shively. For linebacker Hugh Green, a two-time Pro Bowler and Tampa Bay's first-round pick in 1981, the frustration boiled over. In an interview with the United Press International, Green said he was "just trying to survive the season."

Green couldn't even do that. He asked for a trade. Culverhouse said no. Green then staged a one-day walkout from practice and was fined. His unhappiness became a nagging subject. Finally, just five games into the season, Green was traded to Miami for two 1986 draft picks.

"When the Bucs let Doug (Williams) go, that was a bad sign," Green said. "They made me feel cheated."

That's how the Bucs felt after their ninth consecutive loss. They drove into field-goal range while trailing the New York Giants 22-20, but were penalized for holding. Steve DeBerg immediately threw an interception.

"Some guy in Newark threw the flag from the airport," said Bucs offensive lineman Sean Farrell, the guilty party. "The guy

A Bucs fan wears a bag over his head, which became a sight all too common during Tampa Bay's 14 consecutive losing seasons. (AP/WWP)

never takes the flag out of his pocket unless the game is on the line and he's got money on it."

The following day, Farrell apologized for his comment.

Tampa Bay broke through with a 16-0 victory against the St. Louis Cardinals. It was the franchise's first shutout since 1979, but it was not indicative of a defense that had turned the corner.

The very next week, the Bucs lost to the New York Jets 62-28. Never before in NFL history had a team surrendered that many points after registering a shutout. From zero to 62 ... in one week.

The Bucs (2-14) had the draft's No.1 pick for the fifth time in franchise history. But contrary to popular belief, even that was a can-miss proposition.

We're Talkin' Baseball

The Bucs immediately targeted Auburn running back Bo Jackson, the Heisman Trophy winner, who also played baseball and was projected as a major-league prospect. "No way you could pass him up," Bennett said.

In March, Jackson flew to Tampa on Culverhouse's private plane for a physical. Big mistake. It violated a Southeastern Conference rule, and the league automatically recognized him as a professional, thus ending his eligibility for Auburn baseball. Some later wondered if it had been a calculated move, trying to dissuade Jackson from pursuing baseball.

Culverhouse denied the conspiracy theory. "If we take him and he plays baseball, you can all call me a fool," he said on the eve of the NFL draft.

Fool.

After listening to trade offers, the Bucs selected Jackson, who emerged on stage to shake hands with Commissioner Pete Rozelle and smile for the cameras. He did not, however, commit to football. Some Bucs officials got nervous.

Culverhouse, undaunted, pledged he would make Jackson the highest-paid rookie in NFL history. But Jackson, after a visit to Tampa that included fishing and dinner with several Bucs players, was unimpressed with the franchise.

Jackson, taken in the fourth round by the Kansas City Royals, declined Tampa Bay's reported five-year, $7-million contract offer and chose baseball. In a news conference, Jackson said he was done with football. He was tired of waking up sore each morning.

In fact, he simply didn't want to play for Tampa Bay.

So a sinking franchise, coming off a 2-14 season, got nothing for its No. 1 overall draft pick. Nothing except ridicule. Culverhouse tried to put a happy face on his disappointment, saying he had listened to a Dionne Warwick tune—"That's What Friends Are For"—on his drive to One Buccaneer Place.

"Keep smiling ... keep shining," Culverhouse recited in sing-song fashion to a stunned press corps.

By September, Jackson was playing in the big leagues and hit one of the longest home runs in the history of Royals Stadium. In the 1987 NFL draft, Jackson was taken in the seventh round by the Los Angeles Raiders. Wasted pick? Nope. Jackson reversed field and signed with the Raiders, saying football would become his "hobby."

Jackson played four half-season stints for the Raiders, rushing for 5.4 yards per carry in 38 games. He even made the Pro Bowl once. Dual-sport proficiency transformed him into a marketing phenomenon—remember the "Bo Knows" Nike commercial, where he traded guitar riffs with Bo Diddley?—and one of the world's most recognizable athletes.

"I chose another route and that's just the way it is," Jackson said in 2000 during a visit to Tampa, years after he retired from sports due to a degenerative hip. "I wasn't comfortable coming here to play. Not only that, but at the time there were even players here who said, 'Man, you don't want to come here.' So when you've got people already on the team telling you that ..."

Bennett pushed on, claiming it was just another obstacle to overcome. Years later, he admitted it was an insurmountable blow.

"It would have taken more than Bo to turn our team around, but he would have been the centerpiece," Bennett said. "I was assured that we would sign him, but things went downhill. When your football team is down that far, you can't make a guy the first pick in the entire draft and not sign the son of a gun."

The Last Days of Leeman

Jackson's baseball defection wasn't the sole reason for Tampa Bay registering its second consecutive 2-14 season in 1986. The Bucs were awful. It was arguably the worst team in franchise history, even more inept than the expansion group.

During a five-week winless stretch, they lost games by an average of 26 points. They surrendered 473 points in 16 games and only had 19 sacks. James Wilder's production took a downturn. Steve Young was miscast as a drop-back passer.

Bennett stunned everyone at midseason with the outright release of tight end Jimmie Giles (a four-time Pro Bowler), wide receiver Kevin House (the franchise's all-time leading receiver) and running back Ron Springs.

Giles said Bennett told him, "In two or three years when the Bucs are in the Super Bowl, he wanted to go with younger players and I probably wouldn't be around anyway."

The Bucs finished the season with seven consecutive losses. There seemed to be a pair of inevitabilities. Tampa Bay again would earn the draft's overall No. 1 selection, and Bennett wouldn't be making that pick.

Fans threw lemons at Bennett—"Lemon" Bennett, get it?—as he ran into the tunnel after the final home game. Following a season-ending 21-17 loss at St. Louis, Bennett said, "I feel like

I'm going to be here. There's not any doubt in my mind about that."

Speculation festered for one week, until Culverhouse's surreal State of the Bucs address. Culverhouse met with Bennett about 90 minutes prior, allowing the coach to make his points for planned improvement. Bennett, believing he was secure, jotted his thoughts on index cards to detail his priorities for the waiting media.

About 15 minutes before emerging at the podium, Culverhouse made his decision. Bennett would be fired. Then he explained it clumsily.

"While my heart tells me that I would like to see Leeman finish the job that he started ... I do not have the strong feeling of comfort that I'd like to have going into the next season," Culverhouse said. "And it's for that reason that I reluctantly, and with great misgivings, announce that I will seek another head coach.

"So Leeman, I say 'thank you.'"

To summarize: You're fired!

Culverhouse then called Bennett to the podium to "say a few words." Very few. Bennett stammered through a half-hearted thanks for the support he had received, but took no questions. He wheeled, hustled out of One Buc Place and drove away.

Culverhouse was left to look ahead. His words were ominous.

"My God," Culverhouse said, "I hope I don't make another mistake."

Tide Rolls Out; Perkins Rolls In

Tampa Bay fans clamored for Steve Spurrier, the Bucs' first quarterback who had become coach of the wide-open Tampa Bay Bandits. Conveniently, he was unemployed following the USFL's collapse.

Culverhouse went another direction. To the University of Alabama, his alma mater, and the steely-eyed glare of Ray Perkins.

Perkins had replaced the legendary Bear Bryant at Alabama, where he went 32-15-1 in four seasons. Prior to that, he was 24-35 in four seasons with the New York Giants, where in 1981 he produced the franchise's first playoff appearance in 18 seasons.

Culverhouse flew to Birmingham, Alabama, to meet with Perkins at a hotel. They stayed up late, discussing details. They slept briefly, then resumed over breakfast. At noon, Perkins accepted the job.

"It was a whirlwind, and I didn't expect that," Culverhouse later said. "I had never been so enamored with a coach. In the movies, they call it body chemistry. I just knew he was the coach I wanted."

Perkins, introduced in Tampa on New Year's Eve, predicted the Bucs "will win in the third year." He was given control of all football operations. Setting the tone for an often-rocky relationship with media and fans, Perkins added, "I'm not here to win any popularity contests."

He was instantly faced with a monumental decision. Tampa Bay had the No. 1 overall draft pick. Vinny Testaverde, the University of Miami's Heisman Trophy-winning quarterback, was available, although the Bucs already had Young and DeBerg. Also on the board: Alabama linebacker Cornelius Bennett, whom Perkins described as "another Lawrence Taylor with a step more speed."

Perkins made his move—Vinny—and it shaped the franchise's direction for nearly a decade. Young was traded to San Francisco for two draft choices, plus cash. It was a major heist, as Young matured into a Hall of Fame-level player with San Francisco.

For better or worse, the Bucs were wedded to Testaverde. Take a guess how it turned out.

Training Camp Blues

Perkins felt holdover Bucs were accustomed to a country-club atmosphere, which contributed to the two-season record of 4-28. He demanded that out-of-shape players (and even front-office staffers) lose weight and get into condition.

"When you have players complaining about practice, that it's long and they're tired ... if they're so busy worrying about that crap, then they're not too concerned about winning," Perkins said. "That's what I believe and will stand by it to my grave."

Welcome to Camp Perkins. Three-a-days.

In Tampa, home of 95-degree heat and similar humidity, training camp became somebody's bad joke. For the most part, though, the roster was dominated by young players who didn't know better.

"It was like a concentration camp," Perkins later admitted.

You didn't need to convince the smattering of veterans.

"You can't tell me the way he ran things was good," offensive tackle Ron Heller said, a few seasons after leaving Tampa Bay. "We became a worn-out team."

A Perfect Start—Almost

Testaverde was the rage of 1987 training camp, especially when he began with a three-touchdown exhibition game against Cincinnati. Perkins, though, insisted on slow progress. DeBerg was named starter and blitzed the Falcons for a franchise-record five touchdown passes in a 48-10 victory to open the regular season.

"I expected us to win, but I didn't expect it to be in this fashion," said Perkins, who grabbed a cowboy-style hat from a state trooper and galloped into the locker room with it on his head.

The offense looked radically different, even though it was the same DeBerg who had thrown seven interceptions against San Francisco in the 1986 opener. After a 20-3 road loss at powerful Chicago, NFL players went on strike.

Unlike the 57-day work stoppage in 1982, owners had a strategy. Replacement players were employed. The real Bucs gathered for drills at high school fields. The others?

"We are the Scabaneers," said Tampa Bay replacement player James Ramey.

The Replacements

Ramey and a dozen others were refugees from the old USFL Bandits. As they gathered at a hotel prior to the first team meeting, Chuck Pitcock performed a mock center snap to quarterback John Reaves as both players mugged for the lens of a newspaper photographer. It was fun. It was madness.

The replacements went 2-1—the results still count in the record book—but the experience was semi-professional at best.

One replacement Buc worked for Sears. Another was a UPS driver. Still another worked on the freight docks and played semi-pro football. There was an aerobics instructor, a real estate broker, an aluminum salesman and a bill collector. Two were Hillsborough County deputy sheriffs.

"Some of those guys were horribly out of shape," said Doug Graber, Tampa Bay's defensive coordinator. "One of our linemen comes running out in football pants and a half-shirt. He's got this huge gut. I mean, huge. He's laying on the field stretching. And I'm thinking, 'My gosh, what is going on here? Is this really the NFL?'"

Barely.

"I had been out of football for two years," said Ramey, a defensive lineman. "I was out there at practice, feeling good about myself. The next day I tried to get out of bed and the only thing that didn't hurt on my body was my nose. I knew it was temporary. I was a few weeks from getting booted back to reality."

When the players returned, Tampa Bay's official record was 3-2. The Bucs, at least early on, were a contender.

The Collapse

The Bucs were on the verge of moving to 5-3 and putting themselves in position for a playoff run. But the biggest fourth-quarter collapse in NFL history, and a 31-28 loss to the St. Louis Cardinals, prevented that possibility.

Tampa Bay led 28-3 entering the final period. A half-full Busch Stadium crowd began cheering for the Bucs. Then the inexplicable happened. The Cardinals scored a quartet of fourth-quarter touchdowns. Cardinals quarterback Neil Lomax went from scatter-shot to red-hot. The Bucs played too tight.

When Cardinals linebacker Niko Noga returned a fumble for a touchdown, cutting the margin to 28-17, Bucs safety Rick Woods said, "Probably 40 heads looked up at the clock to see how much time was left."

After the Cardinals took a 31-28 lead, the Bucs had one last chance. DeBerg engineered a last-minute drive and positioned Donald Igwebuike for a final-play 53-yard field-goal attempt and overtime. It fluttered through the damp air and hit the crossbar, then harmlessly bounced back to the field.

"A week ago, we were talking about the playoffs," Woods said. "Now we're scrambling for our lives. How can we honestly talk about [making the playoffs] when you blow a 28-3 lead to the Cardinals? They were a bleeding team ready to be stepped on. We didn't do the job."

The Bucs didn't win again in 1987. Testaverde provided encouragement in his first start, when he passed for a then-NFL rookie record 369 yards in a 44-34 loss at New Orleans. But that couldn't erase the disappointment of eight consecutive losses, a 4-11 finish and the realization that there was a long way to go.

Progress Report: Nada

Culverhouse affirmed his confidence in Perkins following the 1987 season, calling him "my Vince Lombardi." But after a 5-11 season in '88, Perkins was running out of time. In fact, he was described as the NFL's worst holdover coach by *Inside Sports* magazine just before the 1989 season.

"He got the Bucs playing hard quickly, but he overstepped good judgment in his boot-camp training camps," wrote veteran NFL reporter Kevin Lamb. "Older players would have revolted. He's a stubborn, humorless man whose inflexibility shows up on the scoreboard, and he has insulated himself from new ideas with a substandard coaching staff composed of young yes-men."

Perkins was supposed to get his last laugh in 1989. It never happened. He pointed to narrow losses, including home defeats to the 49ers and Packers, which were influenced by late penalties. In reality, the Bucs got what they deserved. His prediction had come true.

They had won in the third year.

Five games.

Again.

With another 5-11 season, pressure intensified on Perkins. "We've got a plan and we're sticking to it, come hell or high water," he said. "We should be a winner next year."

If not?

"Then I'll be coming in here and saying goodbye to you all. But I don't expect that to happen."

The Plan Falls Apart

The 1990 season looked like a winner when the Bucs broke out 4-2. "I think we're over the hump," Perkins said. Instead, it was the same old story.

The woeful Dallas Cowboys, trailing by 10 points in the third quarter, rallied for a 17-13 victory against the Bucs, scoring the winner on Troy Aikman's 28-yard pass to Michael Irvin with 23 seconds to play. Cowboys coach Jimmy Johnson later said that game was the first spark toward consecutive Super Bowl championships in 1993-94.

It also effectively finished off Perkins.

Tampa Bay, laboring down the stretch, lost six straight games. Perkins snapped after a 20-10 loss at Green Bay when a reporter asked if he could keep his job. "I don't have to assess my status with this team," he said with a laser-beam glare.

The following Sunday, after beating Atlanta 23-17 to head into a bye week, Perkins confided in a reporter from *The Orlando Sentinel.* "I think I'm gone," Perkins said. Finally, he made the right call. The next day, he was fired and replaced by mild-mannered receivers coach Richard Williamson as interim head coach.

"Ray Perkins was the head coach and, in any company, if the people don't meet their budget for four straight years, they're out," Culverhouse said of his Vince Lombardi.

The Bucs played pressure-free in a 26-13 win against the Vikings. Testaverde opened the scoring with a 48-yard run. Perkins always preached staying in the pocket, so the play was especially satisfying for Testaverde, who rushed for 105 yards overall. "It was nice to run over to the sideline and not get hollered at," Testaverde said.

Tampa Bay lost its final two games to finish 6-10. Although there were suggestions the Bucs sought big coaching names such as Bill Walsh or Bill Parcells, Culverhouse retained Williamson as the permanent coach. But Williamson received only a two-year contract, an especially short leash.

Another Coach Bites the Dust

When examining the Richard Williamson era in Tampa Bay—if one season can be described as an "era"—there's an obvious question.

Did it really happen? If yet another Bucs team glides through a 16-game schedule (at 3-13), does it make a noise? Williamson, so invisible that he actually was described on network television as "William Richardson," never had a chance.

He was supposed to be the anti-Perkins, a coach who could relate to his players in non-dictatorial style. Culverhouse selected Williamson over Buddy Ryan, who had been fired in Philadelphia, and Bill Belichick, then the New York Giants defensive coordinator who later would win two Super Bowls with the Patriots.

"It was a judgment call," Culverhouse said. "I have been right and wrong before in my judgments."

Williamson was the least expensive option ($300,000 annual salary), as was longtime aide Phil Krueger, who was elevated to general manager. Culverhouse also named his daughter, Gay, as team president. Her initial two contributions? Announcing an increase in ticket prices and saying the uniforms needed some spiffing up.

Williamson was blindsided in training camp, with lengthy holdouts by offensive tackle Charles McRae, the first-round draft choice, and cornerback Wayne Haddix, a Pro Bowler.

The Bucs lost their first four games by a total of 13 points, then things went downhill. Tampa Bay's offense had season-long struggles, surrendered a team-record 56 sacks and led the NFL in turnovers with 47. Many of the players who had lobbied for Williamson took advantage of his laid-back style which made for an undisciplined locker room.

The season finale was fitting as the 2-13 Bucs and 1-14 Colts met at Tampa Stadium. The Bucs won 17-3, but who couldn't predict what was ahead?

Williamson was fired.

"We didn't win enough games," Williamson said. "I think I could have turned it around in another year. If I had been in (Culverhouse's) shoes, I would have kept me. But I wasn't in his shoes."

In fact, Williamson was alone at the news conference to announce his dismissal. Culverhouse, working behind the scenes, already was hot-footing it toward a much bigger name—Bill Parcells.

The Done Deal Gets Undone

Things moved quickly, and Culverhouse was on the verge of making Parcells, a two-time Super Bowl winner with the New York Giants, coach of the Bucs. Parcells, who had taken a year off from football and entered broadcasting for NBC-TV, was offered control of football operations, plus the league's highest salary (five years, $6.5 million).

Parcells laid out a list of 38 demands. The Bucs agreed to every one.

A source close to the negotiations told *The Tampa Tribune* "it's a done deal."

But by the following day, it was undone. In a late-night telephone call, Parcells told Culverhouse he was backing out.

That left a teary-eyed Culverhouse to preside over a hastily called news conference.

"We were all set to execute the contract and we now feel as though we were jilted at the altar," Culverhouse said. "I'm still at the altar and, for what it's worth, there was no honeymoon."

Parcells denied talks had ever gotten that far, and vaguely said he couldn't find the proper comfort level to move forward.

End of story? Not exactly.

Six days later, Parcells contacted Culverhouse, saying he wanted to be reconsidered. By then, Culverhouse had begun to navigate through other interviews, most notably with Sam Wyche (recently fired in Cincinnati), Ryan (still out of work) and Mike Holmgren (the San Francisco offensive coordinator, who eventually landed in Green Bay).

Culverhouse gave a final audience to Parcells, but this wasn't an interview. This was payback. An opportunity to spurn the spurner.

Stephen Story, one of Culverhouse's representatives, delighted in telling reporters that Culverhouse "just couldn't find the proper comfort level to move forward" in renewed talks with Parcells.

The head games were done. It was time to hire a coach. Culverhouse's choice: Sam Wyche.

The Adventure Begins

In Cincinnati, Wyche was known for no-huddle offenses, confrontations with officials, clever quips and wacky behavior. "I'm about half nuts," Wyche said. But he also had been a Super Bowl coach, coming within 34 seconds of a championship in 1989.

He masterfully held his introductory Tampa Bay news conference on the back of a flatbed truck outside Tampa Stadium, with some 200 cheering fans in tow. News conference? No, this was a revival.

Wyche promised a revitalization of Tampa Bay's offense, which had finished 26th in 1991. He retained Floyd Peters as the defensive coordinator for the league's 11th-ranked unit.

"I'm an emotional coach," said Wyche, an eclectic man who in addition to being a head coach was an amateur magician and had a pilot's license. "If you're not enthusiastic doing what you're doing, man, get another job. Life's too short. I'm going to put up or shut up."

The 1992 Bucs were 5-11 for the organization's 10th consecutive losing season, but things were rarely dull.

When the Bucs displayed a disturbing trend of second-half collapses, Wyche insisted on practicing the team's halftime routine. Workouts were halted and halftime was simulated as players trotted into One Buccaneer Place for a 12-minute rest. Stools were set up for players to gather around and listen to critiques by assistants.

The Bucs began 3-1 and had a home game with 9 1/2-point underdog Indianapolis. At high tide, Wyche hit a low point, mysteriously ripping into his team following a lackluster practice. He suggested his team could be blown out if it wasn't careful. Strange words. Predictable result. Colts 24, Bucs 14.

The motivational tactics grew more bizarre at midseason when Wyche pulled his assistants off the field, leaving players to extend practice and lead drills on their own.

After a 5-11 finish, Wyche was asked how he watched the playoffs. "From a distance," he said.

Couldn't Get Over the Hump

Testaverde, a lightning rod for six years, opted for free agency prior to the 1993 season and signed with Cleveland. Meanwhile, offensive tackle Paul Gruber, who had played every snap for five seasons, held out until midseason.

Wyche said there would be "no excuses, no regrets, no alibis" as the season began. But the offense labored. There wasn't a triggerman—DeBerg, now a graybeard, was replaced by inexperienced Craig Erickson at quarterback—and the running game averaged 3.2 yards per carry. The Bucs scored one touchdown—one!—all season in the first quarter.

Undue pressure was placed on the defense, which had acquired Hardy Nickerson, a free-agent linebacker from Pittsburgh. Nickerson immediately caused a stir with his frenzied work habits and penchant for getting in the face of teammates he felt were underachieving.

Slowly, the Bucs were building leadership. But another 5-11 season looked like more of the same. Wyche pointed to positives, specifically a late-season 17-10 win at AFC powerhouse Denver. The Bucs also defeated Chicago at home 13-10, after which Wyche was moved to say, "Here's a chance to affect the playoffs. We're not going to be in those playoffs this year. We will next year."

Sounded like a guarantee.

After reading it in print, Wyche backtracked. "Nobody has ever guaranteed a thing that was in his right mind or thinking clearly," Wyche said before the 1994 season.

Wyche had concerns off the field, as well. Culverhouse, who was diagnosed with lung cancer in 1993, had transferred stock of the Bucs to a revocable trust to ensure business as usual. Culverhouse died just before the 1994 season began, leaving the franchise's fate in the hands of three trustees—Stephen Story, Jacksonville attorney Fred M. Cone Jr., and Jack Donlan of Naples—who announced the franchise was for sale.

Would the Bucs leave Tampa? Would Wyche be retained as coach? These questions dogged the franchise weekly. Following a 14-9 loss at Detroit, in which the Bucs failed to score a touchdown despite two possessions at the Lions' 1-yard line, Wyche said he felt he was going to be fired. The following week at Seattle, officials blew three calls in the final two minutes, leaving the Bucs with a 22-21 loss to the Seahawks and a 2-9 record.

It looked like doomsday. But just when no one expected it, the Bucs registered their first four-game winning streak in 15 seasons. One game remained. A final chance, perhaps, for Tampa Bay to keep its team. For the week leading up to the final game, the city was in a frenzy. With Green Bay coming to Tampa Stadium for the season finale, more than 36,000 tickets were sold in six days. Banners were erected. Speeches were made.

The only thing missing was a victory. Green Bay deflated the Bucs 34-19 and the sellout crowd was left wondering whether the orange-clad team would be known as the Baltimore Bucs when 1995 arrived.

New Day in Tampa Bay

The Bucs' trustees retained Wyche as coach, and that plan remained when Malcolm Glazer, a Palm Beach multi-millionaire, agreed to purchase the franchise for $192 million. The team remained in Tampa, but construction of a new stadium became a front-burner item.

Wyche's focus: He had a job. And it looked like his best team yet.

The starting quarterback was second-year man Trent Dilfer, who played sparingly as a rookie after being taken as a first-rounder from Fresno State. Second-year running back Errict Rhett, who rushed for 1,011 yards despite not cracking the starting lineup until Week Nine, bolstered the backfield.

As the Glazer family's first official act, the Bucs signed free-agent wide receiver Alvin Harper from the Dallas Cowboys, the embodiment of the franchise's advertising slogan: "A New Day In Tampa Bay."

"I think we can start beating our chests a little bit," Wyche said.

On defense, with newly installed General Manager Rich McKay leading the selection process, the Bucs used first-rounders for Miami defensive tackle Warren Sapp and Florida State linebacker Derrick Brooks.

Harper only caught one pass in the exhibition season, and that was near the end of a game with the Dolphins in Orlando. That's when he re-aggravated a left ankle injury. Why was the $10.6-million free agent playing during the final minutes of the last exhibition game? "I don't know whose idea it was," Harper said, "but it was a bad idea."

Good Start; Bad Finish

Harper didn't reappear until the fourth game, when he caught a seven-yard toe-tapping touchdown pass from Dilfer against Washington, then promptly was ejected for bumping an official while lobbying for the call.

Tampa Bay's 14-6 victory began a four-game winning streak. There was high drama from place-kicker Michael Husted in a 19-16 triumph against Cincinnati. He salvaged a moribund offensive effort on his 53-yard field goal with 29 seconds remaining.

"I know you're gonna write the word 'ugly' in your headlines," Wyche said. "Just don't misprint 4-dash-2."

The following week at home against Minnesota, on a brilliant afternoon for Dilfer (24 of 37 for 249 yards, no interceptions), it was Husted again with a 51-yarder in overtime to defeat the Vikings 20-17.

Wyche's first word in the postgame news conference:

"YA-HOO!"

Five-dash-two.

Gruber chose a more analytical route.

"We're getting it done," he said. "I don't know how, but we're getting it done."

But the season was fragile. The Bucs threw away their momentum with a disappointing 24-21 home defeat to Atlanta. Three consecutive losses made the record 5-5, then the Bucs climbed above .500 with a 17-16 win against expansion Jacksonville.

The Bucs wouldn't see .500 again until the 14th week, an ESPN Sunday night game with Green Bay. The Bucs won 13-10 in overtime, again getting a dramatic game-winner from Husted.

Afterward, Wyche spent 10 minutes of his postgame news conference criticizing the media for "negative" coverage. Wyche specified an article in *The St. Petersburg Times* that morning. It anonymously quoted Bucs players and coaches, who essentially said Wyche had lost his grip.

"Lies are lies," Wyche said.

Fans apparently weren't happy with Wyche, either. A banner appeared using the ESPN moniker—"Eliminate Sam's Play-calling Now"—before it was removed by Tampa Stadium officials.

Dilfer's relationship with Wyche hit bottom in a 37-10 season-finale loss to Detroit. Dilfer, who had been twice pulled from previous games because of what Wyche termed "exhaustion," was benched in the second quarter for Casey Weldon. Dilfer threw his arms up in puzzlement as he approached the sideline.

Afterward, Wyche said he planned all along to play Weldon. He said quarterbacks coach Turk Schonert was told to relay that message. One problem: Schonert never told Dilfer.

"Absolute lousy communication," said Wyche, who exited the stadium to a chorus of fans chanting, "Sam Wyche Sucks!"

Of the 7-9 finish, Wyche said, "It was a good run for this team."

Yeah, for a circus, according to Dilfer.

"I was waiting for the trapeze to swing down," said Dilfer. "I totally disagree with how it was handled. If I was doing that, I wouldn't leave it to somebody else to take care of the communication. I'd take care of it myself."

Harper, the face of the franchise's commitment to improvement, was often surly and rarely made a significant difference. By season's end, he was hinting at retirement.

Few would have noticed.

After the holidays, Wyche was fired.

"This team is far better than it was four years ago when we started," said Wyche, who was 23-41 with the Bucs. "A good man will come in here and reap some of the benefits of the hard work we put in."

The future wasn't that simple. Would a new stadium be approved? Would the franchise move? Who would become the head coach?

"Understand that the stadium issue ties directly into winning football games," McKay said. "The coach issue ties into winning. The Glazers bought this football team and said the first priority is winning. If that means it's in the best interest of this team to change coaches, we'll change coaches."

To whom would the Glazers turn?

Chapter 7

RESPECTABILITY—
AND BEYOND

Just a Football Coach

Heading into the 1996 season, the Bucs had established the start of a foundation. The presence of defensive tackle Warren Sapp and linebacker Derrick Brooks would pay off handsomely in time. The 1995 Bucs began 5-2 and, early on, had the look of a playoff team while ending the franchise's string of double-digit losing seasons.

But there were issues. The Bucs were embroiled in a contentious battle to build a stadium. The team's local popularity had eroded. Its national reputation could be described succinctly: loser.

For the fifth time in 11 years, the Bucs were searching for a head coach. General manager Rich McKay sought a huge name. But Jimmy Johnson went to the Miami Dolphins. Steve Spurrier stayed at the University of Florida.

So McKay focused on Tony Dungy, the Vikings' defensive coordinator, who had interviewed for four other NFL head-coaching jobs. The word on the street was that Dungy didn't interview well. He was too soft spoken, they said.

"He should've had a job before," McKay said. "Even in our case, he wasn't going to sell us tickets. He wasn't going to make the new stadium happen. He wasn't going to make the city instantly like us again. He was one thing. He was just a football coach."

A Man of Faith

When Dungy was being recruited out of Jackson, Michigan, he told his mother, "I don't want to play for a coach who yells and screams at me. I just don't think that's necessary."

That became Dungy's style. He rarely raised his voice. He stood on the sideline with a stoic expression, arms folded. He followed the lead of his former coach with the Steelers, Chuck Noll, who emphasized teaching and practice-field execution.

"You can't allow coaching to consume you," Dungy said. "Or else you'll flame out, you won't last. I'm an upbeat person, because I know that Christ is working through me. I have a mission on earth. But then I'm going to heaven."

Dungy worshipped privately, but often wore a cross on his jacket lapel or a T-shirt from a Christian organization. He didn't use profanity and sought to hire assistant coaches with a similar approach.

Throughout his athletic career, Dungy had seen the rise of Christianity in the locker room. He also knew non-religious observers derided post-touchdown prayers as public displays of false righteousness.

"I'm not going to stop someone on the street and say, "If you don't change your lifestyle, you're going to hell," Dungy said. "If Magic Johnson uses his career to further AIDS awareness, we as a society tend to think that's good. So if I have a religious experience and want to use my career to further Christian awareness, why is that bad?"

The Bucs, so accustomed to not having a prayer in the NFL, now had a widely respected leader and a firm plan.

Passing the Test

Dungy's 1996 offense was initially crippled by a season-ending knee injury to Horace Copeland, the continued inefficiency of Alvin Harper and the holdout of workhorse running back Errict Rhett, who wanted a new contract. The heat was turned up on quarterback Trent Dilfer, who got off to a dismal start.

The Bucs were 1-8 with the Raiders coming to town. On the players' day off, two Bucs blew off an autograph session. A little thing. But something very big to Dungy.

When players reported, Dungy didn't address the game plan. The Raiders were put on the back shelf. Like a disappointed father, he spoke about the autograph session. That, he said, is why this team isn't winning. Nothing would change unless they were accountable.

The scolding made an impression.

The Bucs won five of their last seven games, starting with an overtime win against the Raiders. The following week at San Diego, the Bucs brought in a 10-game road losing streak and 12 consecutive West Coast defeats.

Earlier that day, Sapp and Brooks were watching ESPN's pregame show. Chris Berman and crew were having a marvelous time at the expense of the "Yucks."

"People were always making fun of the franchise, but somehow we just decided we'd had enough," Sapp said. "They said one of the guys in the studio could throw the next four passes off Tom Jackson's head, get the next two picked off, complete one and still have a higher quarterback rating than Trent had at the time. They all laughed.

"I looked at Brooks. He looked at me and said, 'We got to do something about this.' I said, 'Damn right we do. They're not doing us like this. You're not gonna call me the Yucks. To hell with that disrespect. It's over.'"

That was turnaround day. The Bucs rallied for a 25-17 victory against the Chargers. Dilfer had his best day as a pro, completing 30 of 40 passes for 327 yards.

By the season finale, a 34-19 victory against Chicago at Tampa Stadium, the Bucs were 6-10, but felt like a playoff team.

"We plan on this being the last Christmas we rest," Bucs linebacker Hardy Nickerson said. "It's not how you start a season, it's how you finish. Let's play 16 more games right now."

Making a Statement

San Francisco at Tampa Bay. That was the 1997 opener. One franchise at the top, usually contending for the Lombardi Trophy. Another serving as the butt of jokes.

"In the past, your sense of urgency was to learn the playbook or keep a job," Bucs center Tony Mayberry said. "We're trying to instill some urgency here. It's changing."

The Bucs broke out their pewter helmets, then showed their new look was about more than uniforms.

On a brutally hot afternoon, Sapp set the tone by knocking out 49ers quarterback Steve Young with a concussion on San Francisco's fifth play. It was Sapp again in the second quarter, corralling wide receiver Jerry Rice on an unsuccessful reverse. Rice suffered a knee injury that put him out for most of the season.

Sapp's massive afternoon: 11 tackles, 2 1/2 sacks, two Hall of Fame KO's.

Still, the 49ers led 6-0 at halftime. When the Bucs threatened to take the lead, but Patrick Hape fumbled at the San Francisco 4-yard line, it looked like the close-but-no-payoff result of seasons past.

"In the old days, we would've had a loss, maybe even a blowout loss," Dilfer said. "But this team is built to keep games close and win in the fourth quarter. It was different."

Patiently, Tampa Bay cut the lead in half on Michael Husted's 40-yard field goal, then surged ahead 10-6 on Dilfer's one-yard pass to tight end Dave Moore. That was a nervous margin, particularly when Young was re-inserted. First down: Young was sacked by Nickerson. Second down: Young's pass was intercepted by cornerback Tyrone Leggett, setting up Husted's tack-on field goal.

Tampa Bay 13, San Francisco 6. Things were different.

"Tyrone Leggett," Bucs vice president Joel Glazer said years later. "That play he made. That's when I started to know. We had turned a corner."

That was evident at Dungy's day-after news conference. "It's not a euphoric-type situation," Dungy said. "We're 1-0."

On the Fast Track

The Bucs finally were equipped to build a winning streak. They had a long-missing element—speed.

It mostly came from five-foot-eight running back Warrick Dunn, a first-round pick from Florida State. Dunn's selection as the 12th overall pick was criticized by some because he was perceived as a spot player. Dungy and McKay didn't see it that way.

"A difference-maker," McKay said.

"High character, dependable, a guy you want in tough situations," Dungy said.

Dunn outdid Barry Sanders by rushing for 130 yards and a six-yard score in Tampa Bay's 24-17 win at Detroit. That was followed by a 101-yard performance—and a game-clinching 52-yard touchdown run—in a 28-14 victory at Minnesota.

When the Miami Dolphins came to Tampa for a nationally televised Sunday night game, the Bucs put away a 31-21 victory with Dunn's 58-yard scamper on a screen pass.

The Bucs, predictably flat the following week, gained just 161 yards of offense against the Arizona Cardinals and needed a few miracles. The Bucs went ahead 19-18 when Dilfer's fourth-and-six crossing route pass to Karl Williams turned into a 31-yard touchdown pass. Arizona's Kevin Butler missed a 47-yard field-goal attempt in the final minute.

"We are for real," Sapp said.

The Bucs (5-0) had matched the best start in franchise history.

The pace slowed, preventing the Bucs from winning the NFC Central Division race after being swept by Green Bay. But along the way, they blasted New England 27-7 when the Patriots didn't get their initial first down until the third quarter.

They clinched a winning season with a 20-8 road triumph against the New York Giants. On the game's pivotal play, the Giants sent Tyrone Wheatley up the middle on fourth-and-one from the Tampa Bay 47-yard line.

No gain.

"We took that as an insult," safety John Lynch said. "To run straight ahead, it's not going to happen anymore."

The Bucs finished as a 10-6 wild-card team and secured a home playoff game with a 31-15 victory against Chicago.

A Long Time Coming

The Bucs hadn't hosted a playoff game since the 1979 NFC Championship Game—when Dungy's playing career was winding down and many of Tampa Bay's key players were children.

The final football game played at Tampa Stadium was against Central Division rival Detroit and Barry Sanders, who had rushed for 1,998 yards in 17 career games against the Bucs.

"Take two aspirins and start watching the film," Dungy said. "It's like playing against Michael Jordan and the Bulls."

Bucs coach Tony Dungy celebrates following Tampa Bay's 20-10 NFC playoff victory against Detroit in 1997. (The Tampa Tribune)

Defensive coordinator Monte Kiffin, before showing highlights of Sanders, wrote "Contain 20" on an overhead projector. His players protested. Strike that word, they said.

Stop Barry Sanders. That was the goal.

That's what they did.

The Bucs held Sanders to 65 yards on 18 carries in a 20-10 victory. The Tampa Stadium crowd was electrified.

"We were tired of hearing about Barry," Nickerson said. "We gang-tackled all day. We had 11 guys on him all day."

Tampa Bay's offensive linemen were heroes of a 17-play, 89-yard drive in the second quarter, which culminated in Dilfer's nine-yard TD pass to Copeland. "It seemed like it was a 1,000-play drive," Mayberry said.

Regardless of the play count, a lengthy drive kept it away from Sanders. In the third quarter, Alstott's thunderous 31-yard TD run put the Bucs up 20-0 and left it for the defense.

Afterward, fireworks lit up the night. Sapp ran around the field, waving a giant Bucs flag.

"I have chills," Brooks said.

"There are no words to describe the feeling we have right now," Nickerson said.

Dungy had a few.

"On to Green Bay," he said.

Falling Short

Conditions for the NFC Divisional Playoff Game at Lambeau Field—28 degrees, wind chill of 11, some freezing drizzle—weren't favorable.

The passing game was dreadful (Dilfer was just 11 of 36 for 200 yards). But the Bucs cut it to 13-7 in the third quarter on Alstott's six-yard run, which finished a 94-yard drive. Green Bay answered with a touchdown drive of its own. The Bucs remained in the deep freeze and fell 21-7. A memorable season was over.

The Packers moved on.

But the enduring story was Tampa Bay's defense, particularly the inspired play of Sapp, who had seven tackles, three sacks and forced two fumbles.

More than anything, though, he displayed a toe-to-toe attitude that ignited a personal rivalry of respect with Packers quarterback Brett Favre.

Favre got up woozy, thinking his nose was broken. Sapp chimed in: "Hey, pretty boy! What's wrong?" Favre got in the huddle.

Sapp walked off the field to rest for one play. Favre: "That's right, go take a blow." Sapp wheeled and returned, fuming.

Later in the game, Sapp slammed Favre to the turf. The quarterback, undaunted, looked Sapp in the eyes and said, "Don't you love it?" Sapp, warming to the furiously competitive pace, answered, "Damn right I do!"

"He's wearing green and gold and I'm red and pewter," Sapp said. "We're going to be fighting for a very long time."

The Bucs had arrived. And they weren't going anywhere.

A Season-Long Nightmare

Coming off a playoff berth and preparing for the opening of Raymond James Stadium, there was a buzz surrounding Tampa Bay's 1998 season. It became a year-long hangover.

The Bucs played on the road for all exhibition games and began the regular season 0-2. Finally, their new stadium was completed. It had the feel of a theme park, complete with Buccaneer Cove and a pirate ship that fired cannons and raised flags for the red-zone attack. The Bucs rallied for a 27-15 win against the Chicago Bears, but the season never hit a comfortable stride.

When their postseason hopes looked to be over, they clawed back into contention. On safer ground, they reverted to dismal performances. The Bucs completed an 8-8 season with a 35-0 win at Cincinnati, then clung to desperate playoff hopes.

Those were snuffed out when the Arizona Cardinals (9-7) converted a final-play field goal at San Diego. The Bucs were flying home when hearing the news. In 1997, they were sky-high. This time, their season ended at 35,000 feet.

"When it got to be 21-0 [against the Bengals], I thought, "Where the hell has this been all year?"" said Sapp, who admitted to playing with more weight and less urgency. "We had some flashes of a champion. But also some flashes of an expansion team."

The defense needed to regain its swagger. Most of all, though, the pressure was on Dilfer. Entering the final year of his contract, he needed to improve the league's 22nd-ranked passing offense.

Roller-Coaster Ride

Dilfer's continued inconsistency in 1999 led to a 3-4 start, then the bench. Eric Zeier became the starter but lasted only one game after separating the cartilage in four ribs. Back to Dilfer.

Through 10 games, the Bucs had won twice without scoring an offensive touchdown. They won with six turnovers. They won while allowing seven sacks. Then they learned how to win without Dilfer.

At Seattle, Dilfer broke his right collarbone, giving way to rookie Shaun King, a cool customer from Tulane who hadn't taken an NFL snap. Now he was being asked to preserve a pressurized road victory for a playoff-hopeful team. No problem.

The turnover-free Bucs won 16-3 behind a defense that allowed just 156 yards and forced six takeaways.

"It would be nice if the offense put up a few more points," defensive end Chidi Ahanotu said. "But it's no secret this team is built around us."

King helped by winning four of five starts. The Bucs, once a disappointment at 3-4, won their first division title since 1981 with a 20-6 win at Chicago in the regular-season finale. The Bucs were 11-5 and earned a first-round playoff bye. Everything, it seemed, was breaking just right.

Skin of Their Teeth

If anyone doubted Tampa Bay's status as a team of destiny—or was it just good fortune?—Exhibit A was the NFC Divisional Playoff Game at home. The Bucs defeated the Redskins 14-13 in a game they seemingly had no business winning.

With the Redskins leading 13-0 in the third quarter, the game changed.

Lynch raced to the sideline and picked off a pass from Redskins quarterback Brad Johnson at the Tampa Bay 27-yard line. He stood by his offensive teammates, spiked the ball, then raged: "Do something!"

"John's emotion was incredible," Kiffin said. "Everyone felt it."

The offense got in position on a pass interference call to the Washington 11-yard line. From the 2, Alstott made a determined run that was best described on the official play-by-play sheet.

M. Alstott left end for 2 and touchdown, runs right, finds no hole, tries middle, bounce outside left for TD.

It was 13-7. Next, the rally turned truly ridiculous. After recovering a fumble, the Bucs needed 10 plays—some of them downright bizarre—to score the game-winner. On third-and-three, King was pulled down and fumbled before hitting the turf. Dunn immediately scooped it and ran for 13 yards and a first down at the 17.

"When we got that one, I thought it might be our day," Dungy said.

It was. Following a fourth-down conversion, King delivered the winning touchdown pass while falling backward after getting slammed by a blitzing Ndukwe Kalu. King released the ball in time for tight end John Davis to grab a one-yard touchdown.

Washington had a last-gasp 52-yard field goal attempt, but Dan Turk's snap dribbled back to Johnson, the holder, and he was nailed by Floyd Young.

"I think they could've played all night and they wouldn't have beaten us," Kiffin said. "If they would've gotten that field goal off, it would've hit the goal post and bounced back. Our defense wasn't going to let us lose."

The Bucs were one victory away from Super Bowl XXXIV. How did they get that far? Much credit went to Tampa Bay's defense, which limited Washington, the NFL's No. 2-ranked offense, to 157 yards.

Otherwise, Dunn kept it simple: "It was meant to be."

Heavy Underdogs

Few people gave the Bucs a reasonable chance in the NFC Championship Game. Their opponent, the St. Louis Rams, was coming off a 13-3 regular season in which they scored 526 points (third best in NFL history). The Rams displayed their dizzying pace in a 49-37 divisional playoff victory against the Vikings. No defense had figured out how to slow down Rams quarterback Kurt Warner, the league MVP.

The Bucs were 14-point underdogs.

"You dismiss the hype and concentrate on playing the game on the field," Dungy said. "Do you remember point spreads from the last few Super Bowls? No, you remember who won and what they did to win. All the buildup stuff gets forgotten."

Well, most of it.

Two days prior to the game, the teams appeared separately at a news conference in St. Louis. The Rams were casual, loose and somewhat arrogant. The Bucs arrived in suits, all business, unwilling to reveal much.

Rams receiver Isaac Bruce, munching on a sandwich as he addressed the national media, said he was unimpressed by Tampa Bay's secondary.

"They play a lot of cover-two [zone defense]," Bruce said. "I feel if they could do a satisfactory job of covering, they'd be in man to man." Bruce also implied that Lynch's reckless hitting style could be copied by most anyone.

Those comments were soon relayed to Lynch.

His eyes narrowed.

"Isaac Bruce said that?" said Lynch, clutching the lectern. "There's no doubt about it. They're very confident. They feel good about themselves. Good for them. We don't have to justify why we do what we do because we do it well."

The Bucs didn't blink. Inside, they were churning.

Almost Super

Impartial football fans rejoiced when the Rams emerged from a defensive choke-hold and turned back the ugly-duckling Bucs, 11-6. But for fans of great defense, this game was a beauty.

The Rams escaped on Warner's 30-yard third-down scoring pass to Ricky Proehl—just inside the lunging reach of Bucs cornerback Brian Kelly—with 4:44 remaining.

King nearly drove the Bucs to a winning TD, but the drive fizzled when an apparent 12-yard reception by Bert Emanuel, down to the St. Louis 23-yard line, was overturned by an instant-replay review.

"We held that team without a touchdown for 55 minutes," Dungy said. "They moved the ball at will all season. It may never happen again, against a team like that, in a game that big."

Not everyone had similar enthusiasm for the defensive artistry.

"Eleven to six. That isn't a pro football score. It's a work shift at state government," wrote Art Thiel of *The Seattle Post-Intelligencer.*

"You wonder how long the best defense in football can stand to stay in this marriage," wrote Michael Wilbon of *The Washington Post.* "Any offense at all and the Buccaneers, once symbolic of losing in America, would have been making the trip to the Super Bowl."

After a St. Louis turnover on the first play from scrimmage, King had receiver Jacquez Green open in the end zone on second and goal from the Rams 7. He threw behind Green—incomplete.

Leading 6-5, the Bucs went for a fourth-and-three play from the Rams' 35. King's apparent 23-yard completion to Emanuel on a crossing play was negated by a delay penalty. "I thought I had gotten it off with one second (on the play clock), but I'll have to live with that," King said.

Although the goal was to keep the Rams on a long field, the Bucs carelessly opened it up on third and 11 from the 50-yard line as the fourth quarter wound down. King's high floater for Dunn was picked off by Rams cornerback Dre Bly, setting up the winning touchdown drive.

It was a borderline criminal fate for the Tampa Bay defense, which flew to the ball and set an early tone. In the first quarter, Brooks slammed into Rams receiver Torry Holt as he crossed the middle, bruising his ribs and causing him to spit up blood on the sideline.

Only the late touchdown pushed the Rams past 300 total yards. But the throw was perfect and so was the play call. On third and four, Proehl was running a fade route, and Warner was coming his way if the Bucs blitzed. Before the snap, Proehl and Warner both saw Bucs free safety Damien Robinson creeping to the line.

Warner's pass beat the Velcro-like coverage of Kelly and the onrushing help of Lynch.

"It was the best defense we've ever played," was how Lynch remembered the game. Offensive players had different memories.

"People kept asking how long we could continue to put the defense in positions like that and have them carry us," Emanuel said. "The bottom line is we got exposed."

The Catch (Or Non-Catch)

In the game's aftermath, the controversial play to Emanuel was heavily discussed in Tampa. It would've given the Bucs two shots from the St. Louis 23 (and more opportunities if they earned a first down) with 47 seconds to play. Given their offensive struggles, it wasn't a sure bet for Tampa Bay to reach the end zone.

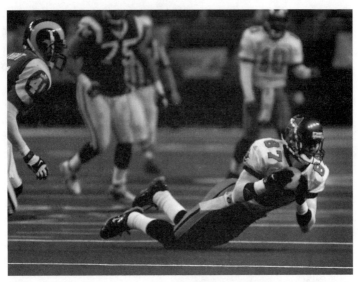

This catch by Bucs receiver Bert Emanuel pulled Tampa Bay to the St. Louis 23-yard line in the closing minute of the 1999 NFC Championship Game. But after reviewing the instant replay, officials ruled against the Bucs and the catch was overturned. The Rams went on to win the game and reach the Super Bowl. (The Tampa Tribune)

But referee Bill Carollo, after checking the replay, ruled that Emanuel used the ground to aid his catch. That made it third down at the 35, prompting desperate measures.

Dungy didn't buy the replay reversal. Neither did King. In the Fox broadcast booth, Pat Summerall and John Madden couldn't understand why the play was overturned. As for Emanuel? "I know I caught it. I caught it clean. It killed our momentum. It was a shock."

Jerry Seeman, then the NFL's director of officiating, said the ruling prompted several venomous e-mails and telephone calls to his office. It also received a series of envelopes with Tampa postmarks. No letters included. Just the same small contents.

Screws.

Shaking Things Up

In the aftermath of late-season offensive drudgery, Dungy initially said he planned no changes on his staff. Mike Shula, the much-maligned offensive coordinator, would stay.

"Everybody thinks that making a coaching change is the way to go," Dungy said. "Most times, it has been my experience that you're just masking other difficulties. I think it's wrong."

But at the Pro Bowl in Hawaii, where the Bucs staff was coaching the NFC team, Shula was fired. Even those who wanted him gone—Shula's offenses never surpassed the league's No. 22 ranking—realized it was a public-relations nightmare.

Dungy was true to his initial word. He didn't want to fire Shula. But ownership, frustrated with offensive inefficiency, forced him to make the move. "The timing is bad, I know," Dungy said, rather uncomfortably. "But we did what we felt like we had to do."

A few seasons removed from the firing, Dungy said he considered resigning on the spot. But his priority was getting the Bucs back into Super Bowl contention for the 2000 season. The moves were fast and furious.

The Bucs opted not to re-sign Dilfer, thus handing the starting job to King, virtually without competition. Les Steckel of the Tennessee Titans, coming off the Super Bowl, was hired as offensive coordinator.

The Bucs traded two first-round draft choices for disgruntled Jets wide receiver Keyshawn Johnson, who was given an eight-year, $56-million contract. Clearly, the Bucs would have a different look on offense. The challenge was getting different results.

The Illusion of Improvement

With the Super Bowl set for Raymond James Stadium, T-shirts circulated around Tampa: "Super Bowl XXXV: Just Another Home Game."

Or so it seemed.

The 2000 Bucs began 3-0—*Sports Illustrated* actually floated the possibility of an unbeaten season—but were promptly shaken by a four-game losing streak, in which the defense surrendered 46 points in the fourth quarters.

The Bucs climbed back into it by winning seven of their next eight games. Steckel's expected innovations had given way to conservatism, predictable passing and between-the-tackles running. It was working, although some wondered how. The Bucs had just 221 yards of offense in a 16-13 win at Miami. "If that is a normal team out there," Dolphins coach Dave Wannstedt said, "we're run out of the stadium."

The Bucs clinched a playoff berth with a riveting 38-35 victory against the Rams on *Monday Night Football*. In the locker room, King whooped it up. As usual, he wore his ball cap backward. Dungy spotted him. The front and center coach reached for a hug, but first stopped to turn his ball cap around backward. The quarterback had grown up. The coach showed his proud approval.

The Bucs (10-5) were in the playoffs. But heading into the regular-season finale at Green Bay, they still had a shot to win the NFC Central. And they could finally end the franchise's inexplicable streak of never having won in temperatures below 40 degrees.

With kickoff temperatures at 15 degrees (second coldest in team history), Tampa Bay staged a fourth-quarter rally and set up Martin Gramatica for a 40-yard game-winning attempt with nine seconds remaining. He pushed it right.

Green Bay won the overtime coin toss, ran 10 plays and kicked a game-winning field goal. Yes, the Bucs (10-6) made the postseason. But later in the day, the Vikings lost at Indianapolis. The Bucs had blown their opportunity to win the division, the No. 2 playoff seed and a bye week. Now the Bucs were the No. 5 seed. They were headed to Philadelphia, back into the cold.

Chill-Adelphia

The Bucs, unable to shake the defeat at Green Bay, probably lost before they arrived in Philadelphia for the NFC playoffs. With a heavy snowstorm hitting Philadelphia, they left a day early and had the day-before walkthrough in a hotel ballroom.

The game-time wind-chill factor was 11 degrees at dank Veterans Stadium. Tampa Bay's lifeless offense offered nothing. The defense, which tackled horribly, was nickel-and-dimed by Philadelphia quarterback Donovan McNabb. The Eagles eliminated the Bucs 21-3 and it could have been much worse.

"I was really shivering out there," Ahanotu said. "When you stay on the field that long, you're going to wear down."

"At some point, we stopped bringing our tackling game," Lynch said. "They were falling forward in piles. It wasn't good."

Neither was Tampa Bay's offense.

Leading 3-0, the Bucs had third and 19 from their 25-yard line. Dungy said there was a "breakdown in communication" and Alstott wasn't sent into the game to block in the backfield. So with King dropping, the quarterback's blindside was protected by the ineffective George Hegamin and the diminutive Dunn. Hugh Douglas blew past both players. King was struck from behind. The ball popped loose, and the Eagles recovered.

When Philadelphia scored to lead 7-3, that was it.

That was how low Tampa Bay's offense had sunk. The second half became a lost cause. At one point, McNabb stood over center and laughed at Tampa Bay's defense.

"You can't win a game 3-0," Keyshawn Johnson said.

"We're not a terrible team," Ahanotu said. "We were one or two plays away from starting this thing [playoffs] at home and that could have made all the difference."

King said the Bucs played with no urgency, as if they had a game scheduled for the next week. The Bucs left Philadelphia muttering about what might have been. Soon they would need to address reality.

The offense was languishing. The defense was getting older. Tampa Bay's window of opportunity was closing.

More Changes

After the season, Dungy fired Steckel, meaning the Bucs would have their third offensive coordinator in three seasons. Dungy struggled to explain the move, although it was later learned there was friction between Steckel and other staffers. During Super Bowl XXXV week in Tampa, a *New York Post* report suggested the Glazers had contacted Bill Parcells and Dungy was about to be fired. There never was confirmation of the report's validity, but rumors had begun. And they wouldn't stop.

Quarterbacks coach Clyde Christensen was elevated to offensive coordinator, a move that ultimately spelled the end for Dungy. Ownership fumed, but stood by silently. If it didn't work, there would be accountability.

The Bucs improved by signing free-agent quarterback Brad Johnson and defensive end Simeon Rice. Sapp issued an ultimatum, saying the Bucs would be broken up—players and coaches—if the team couldn't reach the Super Bowl. They needed to move forward.

"If it doesn't happen this year, there's gonna be hell to pay," Sapp told ESPN.

He was right.

Paper Champions

The 2001 Bucs failed to separate themselves from the pack. It didn't take long for players to start grumbling about Christensen's offense. "We practice stuff all week, then we get into games and we don't do [crap]," Green said. "It's just throw to Keyshawn, run Warrick, throw to Keyshawn."

Things disintegrated in a 17-10 home loss to the Pittsburgh Steelers, whose blitz packages baffled rookie offensive tackle Kenyatta Walker. Brad Johnson, who was sacked 10 times, read a brief statement afterward and didn't take questions from reporters.

In the Pittsburgh locker room, there was plenty of talking, particularly from safety Lee Flowers, who dismissed the 2-3 Bucs as "paper champions."

Who could argue?

Fighting Back

Dungy's teams fell into a maddening habit: Slumping at midseason, then gathering momentum for a playoff push. In 1999 and 2000, the Bucs were 3-4, but rallied behind a late-season turnaround.

At 4-5 and headed to St. Louis, the Bucs appeared poised for a Monday Night funeral. *The St. Petersburg Times* reported that Dungy's agent, Ray Anderson, approached the Glazers before the season about a contract extension beyond 2002. Ownership declined. To some, that signaled the end.

Instead, in one of the most inspired efforts under Dungy, the Bucs upset the Rams 24-17, finally mixing effective running with controlled passing. The defense did its part, limiting the Rams to 76 yards rushing and forcing five turnovers.

"That's what we're capable of," Lynch said. "Sometimes you need a win like this to give you that spark or springboard."

Dungy was the calm, even in the face of rumors.

"Whether people think your job's on the line or not really doesn't have anything to do with you winning," Dungy said. "You can't get distracted by it."

The Bucs finished 9-7 and reached the playoffs. But all that meant was another first-round trip to Philadelphia. They were determined to avoid the same dismal result.

They did. It was worse.

The Vultures Circle

"Dungy out if Bucs lose."

That was *The St. Petersburg Times'* banner headline that greeted players as they boarded a flight to Philadelphia. According to the story, the decision had been made. What's more, a tentative agreement was reportedly in place with Parcells.

The Bucs weren't just looking for revenge. They weren't just trying to reach their first Super Bowl. They were playing for Dungy's job.

Those who expected a monumental, save-the-day performance were way off base. The Bucs were bludgeoned 31-9. Brad Johnson had his poorest effort of the season (four interceptions, no touchdowns). The Bucs' offense hadn't scored a touchdown in 12 consecutive quarters in the postseason.

A pointed question was posed to Dungy: Was this his last game with Tampa Bay?

"I don't think so," Dungy said, "but I don't make those decisions. I'm not going to speculate. We don't need a funeral here."

Players vocally supported Dungy, who made the playoffs in four of his last five seasons.

"We have great players," Dunn said. "But we played like an average team."

In a meeting the night before the game, Keyshawn Johnson addressed the team and talked about Dungy. "We can make the decision [about Dungy's future] hard or we can make it easy," he said. "It's up to us."

After the game, surrounded by a pack of reporters, Keyshawn lashed out at teammates that he claimed "laid down," but wouldn't give names.

"If Tony's not the coach, then the guy [Parcells] they're talking about bringing in here, he's not going to put up with this [crap]," Keyshawn said in a tearful tirade. "It's almost like a wildfire. If one guy decides he doesn't want to play, then everybody else doesn't play. We better get some people in here who want to play and get rid of the talkers."

Clearly, something had to change. Christensen's offense was a disaster. The Bucs finished 30th in rushing (only 85.7 yards per game) and were tied for 26th overall (293.4). Keyshawn caught a franchise-record 106 passes, but scored only once. Dunn, now a free agent, was bothered by injuries and had his worst season (2.8 yard average per carry).

"We have to evaluate how we got ourselves into these positions [offensively]," McKay said. "But Tony is our football coach. His record speaks for itself. I can't say it simpler than that."

But it wasn't McKay's decision to make.

The Firing of Dungy

Back home, Dungy spoke in terms of the 2002 season. McKay reiterated that nothing would be discussed until after his 48-hour rule—in place to escape from the season's emotions—had elapsed.

On a Monday night, with Parcells rumors swirling, Dungy was unceremoniously fired, with official word distributed in a three-paragraph news release.

The next day, on the front page of *The Tampa Tribune*, a photograph appeared of Dungy packing his belongings into his truck as rain fell into the gloomy night. Even fans who had tired of Dungy's offensive stubbornness were stunned at the manner of this firing.

"There's never an easy way to do this," Joel Glazer explained the following day in a testy news conference. "It's not pleasant and because it was Tony Dungy, it was downright miserable.

"You can criticize how it happened and what happened, that's fine. But just know one thing: We're in this to win a championship and we're going to do what we think is in the best interest of the franchise to win a championship."

In typical fashion, the ousted Dungy awoke the next morning and participated in a school carpool with neighborhood children. Then he arrived at One Buc Place for his final news conference. As he entered the room, some media members applauded.

"As a boss you have to make decisions," Dungy said. "I've made them and done what I think is best for the team. My boss has made his decision on what he thinks is best for the team."

The Glazers told reporters they hadn't undercut their coach. They hadn't been in contact with Parcells. Later in the day came word: The Glazers had contacted Parcells within hours of the news conference.

The aftermath now seems fairly incredible. Parcells, days away from being named Tampa Bay's coach, backed away from discussions with the Bucs, saying a deal had never been in place. (Postscript: When Parcells was hired by the Dallas Cowboys, the Glazers claimed they *did* have an agreement with him and demanded compensation from the Cowboys. That was rejected by the NFL.)

The Glazers, scrambling, turned to McKay, whose search produced Ravens defensive coordinator Marvin Lewis. Nope, the Glazers said, keep looking. Then the owners conducted their own search, somehow prying loose Jon Gruden from the Oakland Raiders.

Dungy, now with the Indianapolis Colts, could only watch as Gruden's Bucs won Super Bowl XXXVII. Gruden, to his credit, constantly praised Dungy, who wasn't forgotten by his former players.

"Tony taught us how to play and how to conduct ourselves as professionals," Lynch said after the Bucs won the Super Bowl.

"That man freed me up and made me the player that I am," Sapp said.

Questions remained: Had Dungy simply fallen short by one season? Could he have been celebrating a championship if the Glazers hadn't pulled the plug?

"Those are questions nobody will ever be able to answer," cornerback Ronde Barber said. "But Tony got this franchise started in the right direction. That's not up for debate."

Chapter 8

THE OWNERS

They Called Him "Mr. C"

Hugh Culverhouse, the charter owner of the Bucs, died August 25, 1994 at the age of 75 after a 20-month battle with lung cancer. Afterward, details of a secret life unknown to Joy Culverhouse, his wife of 52 years, came to light during a bitter and scandalous family battle over his $350 million estate.

Upon learning through court documents and testimony that her husband had been involved in a series of affairs with other women, Mrs. Culverhouse verbalized her shock.

"I'd like to pull him out of the grave and shoot him."

For that, she'd have to stand in line behind lots of Bucs fans.

The NFL Comes to Tampa Bay

In 1974, the NFL awarded Tampa Bay a franchise and tabbed Culverhouse, a Jacksonville, Florida, tax attorney, as owner. Cost: $16 million.

Culverhouse was lauded for luring John McKay to coach the team and managed to remain above criticism during the 0-26 start. By the 1979 playoff run, Culverhouse had become a popular, yet caricature-like, fixture on the sideline. There was no mistaking the bulbous nose, bright orange sport coat and white shoes.

It was when his checkbook was challenged by quarterback Doug Williams's contract stalemate in 1983 that Culverhouse's reputation for frugality—and the franchise's path to self-destruction—reared itself.

"Winning wasn't important to him," Williams said. "Money was all that mattered."

A telling postscript to the Williams fiasco unfolded nearly 20 years later. In a stunning act of generosity, Culverhouse's son donated $1 million to Williams's alma mater, Grambling State University, where Williams had become head coach.

Grambling officials couldn't help but wonder what Culverhouse's father would have thought of his son's philanthropy.

"When I go to hell," Hugh Jr. said, "I'll ask him."

Tough to Figure

Even those who knew Culverhouse, the businessman, had difficulty getting a read on what motivated him. Money? It was more complicated than that. Culverhouse had lots. For all his miserly ways with the Bucs, his generosity extended to the community made for a curious paradox.

The Pinellas County chapter of the National Foundation of the March of Dimes named Culverhouse its 1978 Humanitarian of the Year. He endowed chairs at Jacksonville University and his alma mater, the University of Alabama, where he was on the boxing team with future Gov. George Wallace. He donated millions to medical research at the University of South Florida.

Culverhouse also had the entire state in mind with regard to professional sports. As a member of the Florida Council of 100, Culverhouse brought the commissioners of the four major professional sports to the state in hopes of enticing expansion—all four are now represented in the state by a combined eight franchises—and was an influential member of the Professional Golfers Association.

Advertising Their Dislike

In 1989, Culverhouse, citing sagging attendance at Tampa Stadium, told an *Orlando Sentinel* reporter that he was considering playing three home games a year in Orlando. The public was aghast. Attendance, fans claimed, reflected the product.

Culverhouse eventually backed off, but the damage was done. One local radio station purchased a billboard near the stadium with the picture of a distinctive piece of hardware next to Culverhouse's name.

Translation: Screw Hugh!

"Actually, the original idea was for a noose," explained WFLZ station manager Dave Macejko at the time. "But the ad company wouldn't go for that."

Culverhouse's reaction?

"Great," he said. "Whether it is a joke or serious or half of each, I hope it continues so that we play games here and they care enough to come out and support us. Whether they throw watermelons at me, fine, just as long as they come out and support us."

The man never wavered from his old-school approach. He wanted one coach to wield all the power and one executive to control the money. Culverhouse believed that was the formula that one day would make the team successful.

He died believing it.

Despite the Bucs' ineptitude, Culverhouse was one of the game's most powerful and respected men. He made a lot of money from all those years of losing, and along the way used shrewd legal skills to make his fellow owners richer.

Said General Manager Rich McKay: "His legacy to the NFL is that he brought the financial aspects of the league out of the dark ages and into the modern age."

The Only Thing Powerful About the Bucs

Culverhouse was born February 20, 1919 in Birmingham, Alabama. There the seeds were sown for a life that friends and colleagues likened to a Southern gentleman; and some players compared to a plantation owner.

His drawl remained with him for life. Culverhouse admitted years later that he used his accent as a form of legal gamesmanship, believing it seduced his opponents into underestimating him.

After a five-year military hitch that included a tour as a pilot in the Pacific, he returned to Alabama, earned his law degree and eventually went to work for the state attorney general. By 1955, following a recall to active duty in Korea, Culverhouse was earning $20,000 per year as an IRS investigator in

Jacksonville. His private practice began in 1956, with offices in Jacksonville, Miami and Tampa.

When Culverhouse joined the NFL at age 57, he was regarded as one of the country's finest tax attorneys and an expert in labor law. It was through the latter that Culverhouse ascended to power among his NFL brethren even while his team, saddled by the lowest payroll and worst facilities in the league, annually played the role of league doormat.

Culverhouse was making more than $10 million per year.

Hugh Culverhouse was considered one of the most astute financial minds in the NFL, although he was thought of as a tightwad when it came to spending money on the Bucs. (The Tampa Tribune)

"You didn't argue with him very often," Stephen Story, a Culverhouse business manager, once said in a court deposition. "I mean, it wasn't a wise thing to do. You made your comments and ducked."

As chairman of the NFL Management Council and member of the league's finance committee, Culverhouse was the brain behind the NFL's defense in a lawsuit brought by the USFL in 1986 that claimed the NFL violated antitrust laws. The upstart league won a judgment in court. Damages awarded: $3. Within a week, the USFL folded.

In 1987, Culverhouse was prominent in the league's decision to use replacements when the players union went on strike. Hiring "scabs" allowed the games to continue, as angry union members demonstrated outside stadiums. Eventually, players crossed picket lines, accelerated negotiations and the season resumed after one of the strangest three weeks in league history.

Culverhouse resigned from both of those power committees in 1990.

"It wasn't until he stopped participating on an active level that people came to appreciate how much he did do and how much good he did for the league," former Management Council Executive Director Jack Donlan said. "I think [former NFL Commissioner] Pete Rozelle would tell you that there was not a major monetary decision made in the league without Hugh's consultation."

Way Before Viagra

Among his harem of mistresses, Culverhouse claimed Susan Brinkley, wife of NBC broadcaster David Brinkley. According to court documents, she received checks from a secret bank account and often accompanied him on his private jet to exotic places.

That was when environmental lobbyist Charlton Ford or country club cocktail waitress-turned-amateur photographer Patricia Smith or other objects of Mr. C's affection weren't around.

All of the women's names came up during the estate trial.

"I think he planned to marry either or both—or he might have become a Mormon," Hugh Jr. said during the trial.

George Sims, a co-pilot on Culverhouse's private jet, testified that he once left the cockpit to go to the bathroom and caught his boss and Smith in the act.

"He had his hands physically inside her blouse massaging her breast," said Sims, who testified that Culverhouse's trysts got to be like "comedy" shows, with employees sneaking women on and off jets. Sims recalled another pilot remarking, "It's like he's got a girl in every port."

Culverhouse Sr. spent his final years trying to convince his wife that creditors were at his door and that no money would be left when he was gone. He asked her to sign a post-nuptial agreement.

"He was sick, and he said that the banks are probably going to take over, and I want you to have something," Joy Culverhouse testified. "And he said, 'You could just end up with nothing because the banks are going to take over. I'm in terrible, dire straits.'"

When she finally did sign in February 1993, the agreement left her with the couple's $2 million condominium, $5 million in cash and $2 million in jewelry. The rest of his $350 million estate went to a trust controlled by Story, Donlan and another business associate.

When Culverhouse died 18 months later, the first check cut from the trust's account was a $150,000 payment to Smith; hush money to keep her from going to the press about their affair.

The End

Sims, the co-pilot, recalled a conversation he once had with Culverhouse about a year before the owner's death. "He wished he could trade his money for my relationship with my family," Sims said in a deposition. "He said, 'I'd trade you my money. Here in later life, I've realized that I have severed relationships with my family that I wish I—if I could give away my money and get that back—I wish I had that back.'"

In his final days, Culverhouse was confined to a bed in a quarantine wing of a Louisiana hospital. According to *The Orlando Sentinel*, he was under 24-hour surveillance, his care left to a rotation of 65 nurses, and his room lined with lead.

Culverhouse was radioactive.

He agreed to play guinea pig for an experimental radiation therapy never tested on humans. It called for daily doses of high-grade iodine more than five times the amount used to treat patients with thyroid cancer. The iodine, which was flown in daily from a nuclear plant in South America, was supposed to attack the hundreds of tumors that ravaged Culverhouse's body. But there were too many, it was too late.

The day Culverhouse died, none of the many women in his life were by his side.

No one from his family was, either.

The New Guy

The second owner of the Bucs figured to come from a pool of three suitors. One of Tampa's wealthiest residents, New York Yankees owner George Steinbrenner, was the sexiest name. He was local and had a track record for success and headlines. Groups headed by Chris Sullivan, founder of the Outback

Bucs owner Malcolm Glazer purchased the franchise for a record $192 million in 1995, an amount regarded as outrageous considering the Bucs history. Eight years later he was hoisting the Lombardi Trophy. (The Tampa Tribune)

Steakhouse chain, and Baltimore Orioles owner Peter Angelos were in the mix. Sullivan wanted to keep the team in town, while Angelos's motives were rooted in moving the team to Baltimore.

Those were the guys Tampa Bay knew about.

Malcolm Glazer lurked in the background.

Having developed a reputation as a "tire kicker" on the sports franchise front, Glazer had pursued the New England Patriots and an expansion team for Baltimore. He'd flirted with buying baseball's San Diego Padres and Pittsburgh Pirates. He was waiting for the right team, the right time, and more importantly, the right deal.

In January 1995, executors of the Culverhouse trust agreed to sell the Bucs to Glazer for $192 million, a record price for a sports franchise in America. Repeat: $192 million for a team that had gone 88-207-1—a winning percentage of .298—during its 20-year history.

After being helped to the microphone by two of his sons at the news conference introducing him as the franchise's new owner, Glazer promised through his Amish-like beard to keep the team in town.

"The Bucs stop here," Glazer proclaimed in his first news conference. "Tampa is going to have this team forever as far as the Glazers are concerned. We're committed to keeping the team here."

Conditions were forthcoming.

Malcolm in the Middle of Everything

Bob Walton was hired by Glazer in 1976 to become general manager of a television station in Columbus, Georgia.

"The first job Malcolm gave me on the day he bought the station was to fire 14 people," Walton told *The St. Petersburg Times*. "He later exercised his right to trim expenses by cutting me off, too."

Gentlemanly and ruthless, shrewd and calculating, Glazer was a self-made millionaire. His rise to financial genius began at the side of his father, a watchmaker, whose parents migrated to the United States from Lithuania in 1915. Abraham Glazer died in 1943, leaving eight-year-old Malcolm as the man of a house that included his mother, four older sisters and two younger twins. His jewelry and watch repair business on a New York military base eventually netted Glazer around $50,000 per year.

When the base closed, Glazer's focus turned to real estate. He purchased several duplexes and trailer parks in Rochester, N.Y. In time, Glazer was drawn to the lure of Wall Street. He bought downtrodden companies, cleaned them up, cut costs and sold them for sizable profit.

Glazer became a heavy stockholder in Formica and Harley-Davidson, seeking to buy both companies. The transactions eventually landed in federal court, where a judge compared Glazer to a "snake in sheep's clothing rather than a wolf in sheep's clothing."

In the 1980s, his diversified empire had hands in restaurants, TV stations, shopping centers, nursing homes, mobile homes, an oil company, a fishing company and a stake in tubas and trombones. But the idea of owning a football or baseball team intrigued him. The notion caught some of Glazer's people by surprise.

As one longtime assistant noted, "I've never even seen him pick up the sports page."

If You Build It, They Won't Go

Glazer didn't wait to let the people of Tampa Bay know that the Bucs needed a stadium. And he had no intention of paying for it.

"We have done our part financially," Glazer said. "We bought the team. We paid a big price. And we need now the cooperation of the community for this stadium."

Tampa Stadium, which had hosted Super Bowls in 1984 and 1991, had outlasted its usefulness. Glazer made it clear that for the Bucs to compete with the rest of the NFL, the community had to build a state-of-the-art facility with club seats and corporate boxes.

"It's not just a sports franchise, it's a wonderful magnet to get people to know about the city and to help the city prosper. It's a civic treasure," Glazer said of his team. "So I'm not even going to think that it's not going to happen. The people who are smart in Tampa Bay know it's an essential ingredient, and that they'll work with us to do it."

Some did, others did not.

It wasn't until well into 1996 that Glazer and city council members agreed to make the stadium part of a $2.7 billion referendum to fund construction of schools, roads and public safety projects.

The bartering reached its contentious apex the night of February 28, 1996, a date Glazer had set as a midnight deadline for his long and ever-growing list of demands to be met. One of those late demands required the first $2 million in profits from parking and concessions at all events in the stadium go to the owner of the football team.

At 11:01 p.m., Glazer looked at his watch and made an announcement to the mayor and a roomful of city and county officials.

"You have 59 minutes," he said.

The deal did not get done that night, but it was in place by the summer, giving the owner's two sons and McKay enough time to begin lobbying efforts. The referendum would go to vote on Septamber 3. If it didn't pass, Tampa likely would lose the Bucs.

On September 1, 1996, the Bucs played the Green Bay Packers in the season opener at Tampa Stadium. How the team fared, many believed, would swing the vote.

Packers 34, Bucs 3.

The referendum passed 53 percent to 47.

On September 20, 1998, Raymond James Stadium, built at a cost of $168.5 million, was christened. Through its first six seasons, all 50 games were sellouts.

Two of those were playoff games.

Clearly, these were not Culverhouse's Bucs.

Fashion Statement

Orange.

For 21 years, that was the color the Bucs wore every fall. Talk about your throwback jerseys, Tampa Bay's should have been thrown back a long time ago, along with the "Bucco Bruce" pirate logo that adorned the helmet.

"To be honest, the orange uniforms never bothered me that much," strong safety John Lynch said. "But the guy on the helmet winking at you? That wasn't very intimidating, if you know what I mean."

The Glazers recognized as much. After all, the term "pastel foot wipes" really didn't invoke a positive image.

"How we looked was the most tangible thing. It may sound crazy, but I think when our players ran out there in those bright orange uniforms, it had an effect on the mental attitude," Joel Glazer said. "It was always a reminder of losing. It just needed to change. And if it was going to show up in every store in America, you wanted it to look right. So we took our time."

After their first season, the Glazers went to work, along with McKay, plus the artists and designers of NFL Properties. Nearly 100 meetings were required before the finished product was approved.

"I vividly remember the key question that drove which way we were going to go," McKay said. "Is this going to be evolution or revolution?"

To find the answer, the Glazers researched pirate history. They wanted authenticity and a rollicking attitude, but they also wanted distinctiveness. They found the latter with pewter, a color that would be unique to the Bucs. They found the former in red, the color of the flag that pirates of the high seas used to fly before an attack. To appease any purists, a narrow orange trim was used as a highlight to the black numbers. Bucco Bruce was replaced by a far more menacing character.

"There's just an overall toughness to the look," Glazer said. "It was exactly what we wanted."

The team unveiled the uniforms in a fashion-show like performance at Tampa's downtown convention centerin 1997. Critics raved.

"Everything's changed from the top of the organization down to the bottom," fullback/model Mike Alstott said. "From colors to logo, it's up to the players to go out and win."

"Pewter Power" was born. Within months, Bucs merchandise, invisible outside the Bay area, soared with sales ranked among the NFL's top 10 teams.

Another Fish Story

Malcolm Glazer's pockets were every bit as deep as his predecessor, except Glazer was more willing to reach into them. He and his sons provided McKay and Dungy all the resources and capital needed to chase a championship.

Dungy deserved the bulk of the credit for the on-field makeover, as the team reached the playoffs four times in five seasons from 1997 to 2001. He also deserved the bulk of the blame for hitching his wagon to a defense-only mentality and a trio of offensive coordinators—Mike Shula, Les Steckel and Clyde Christensen—who lacked creativity.

In 2001, as the Bucs stumbled to a fourth straight 3-4 start, rumors circulated that the Glazer sons had put out clandestine feelers to Bill Parcells. Ten years after leaving Culverhouse at the altar, Parcells had stepped down as coach of the Jets following the '99 season.

On January 12, beneath a cloud of negative speculation and rumors, the Bucs were trashed 31-9 at Philadelphia in the playoffs. It was Tampa Bay's second straight first-round exit at Philly and third straight postseason game without a touchdown.

Two nights later, the only Bucs coach with a winning record was fired. To no one's surprise, Dungy went out with class, even thanking the grounds crew at the press conference announcing his dismissal.

Then the Glazer sons came in the room.

Advised by their public relations director to issue a statement, the Glazers instead tried to answer questions about Dungy's firing and the direction of the team. It was an angry group when the Glazers got there. It was worse when they left.

"We've had no conversations, but we're going to start the search next," said Joel Glazer, who denied any link to Parcells despite media reports. "...You've got to have a lot of respect for a guy like Bill Parcells. So to not think of him would be to not explore all the candidates."

A little more than two hours later, the statement came saying Parcells had officially been contacted.

Wrote *The St. Petersburg Times*: "Raise your eyebrows. Roll your eyes. Shake your head. Then believe whatever you want to believe. In the end it comes down to this. Either the Glazers are classless. Or they are clueless."

When Parcells announced two days later that he would not seek the Tampa Bay coaching job, the Glazers looked like both.

When Jon Gruden emerged at the end of the 36-day coaching search, they looked like geniuses.

They looked even smarter after Super Bowl XXXVII.

Chapter 9

QUARTERBACKS

Unhappy Homecoming

I n 1967, Steve Spurrier won the Heisman Trophy at the University of Florida. Twenty-five years later, he won the first of six SEC championships at his alma mater, a prelude to a school-record 122 victories and a 1996 national title. He's remembered as one of the greatest players and coaches in college football history.

"And the starting quarterback for the losingest team in NFL history," he proudly adds.

Years after commandeering the 0-14 Bucs of 1976, Spurrier still regales audiences with stories of his final NFL season.

"We had a bunch of ragtag players out there, boy," he said. Spurrier fit in.

Three days after the expansion draft, the Bucs traded two scrubs and a second-round draft pick to San Francisco for Spurrier. The PR-driven deal brought Spurrier back to the state and put fans at the ticket windows.

Steve Spurrier (#11), the first quarterback in Bucs history, waits for the play call on the sideline with Coach John McKay in 1976. (The Tampa Tribune)

Spurrier had been the third overall choice in the '68 draft, but spent his first eight seasons as a backup. Though Spurrier held a share of the 49ers' single-game record of five touchdown passes, he'd taken more snaps as a punter.

When the Niners traded for Jim Plunkett, whose Heisman at Stanford was three years fresher, Spurrier became expendable.

"It's like a dream coming true that couldn't come true ... but did," the 31-year-old Spurrier said at the time.

Instead, it became a nightmare that couldn't possibly last an entire season . . . but did.

"It might not have been so bad if we'd won a couple of those close games," Spurrier said. "Not only were the Bucs bad, we were unlucky."

Spurrier completed a respectable 50.2 percent of his passes for 1,628 yards, seven touchdowns and 12 interceptions. His season highlight came against Miami, when he tossed two fourth-quarter touchdowns, only to watch Garo Yepremian boot a field goal in the closing minute for a 23-20 Dolphins victory.

The season lowlights were weekly.

If he wasn't being benched in favor of Terry Hanratty or Parnell Dickinson, Spurrier was running for his life, getting tossed like a doggie toy or arguing with Coach John McKay.

Years later, McKay summed it up like this: "[My] relationship with Spurrier? I had no relationship with Spurrier."

In time, Spurrier said the 1976 experience prepared him for coaching.

"It also gave me some good speech material," Spurrier said.

Like the team meeting when McKay broke into a lecture on the importance of being tough in the trenches. "Games are won and lost at the line of scrimmage, and that's where we're losing our games," the coach said.

"Right about then," Spurrier recalled, "McKay looked to the back of the room and there was one of our offensive lineman, Howard Fest, doing what he usually did when the coaches were talking—he was sound asleep."

Fest!

Yes, Coach.

Where are most games lost?

Right here with the Buccaneers, Coach.

Spurrier chuckles when he tells it. "One of my best stories."

An Unforgivable Miscalculation

The bitter contract squabble and defection of Doug Williams in 1983 was an ugly episode in the short history of a franchise that not only weathered its horrific beginnings, but turned the corner toward respectability. Owner Hugh Culverhouse's unwillingness to meet Williams's demands undermined everything McKay and his players had built.

But as catastrophic as Williams's departure was initially, it worsened as he blazed a trail into NFL history.

During a time when the Iran Hostage Crisis led the nightly news, it was suggested that Williams be sent to the Middle East because he was the only one who could "overthrow the Ayatollah." This was a quarterback whose first throw as a Buc—a 70-yard incompletion—got a standing ovation; who heaved a touchdown pass from the seat of his pants after slipping on a wet field.

His numbers weren't great. It wasn't until his fourth season that Williams completed 50 percent of his passes. In only two of five seasons did he throw more touchdowns than interceptions.

But a difference-maker? The Bucs were 34-36-1 when Williams started and 3-31 over the first seven seasons when he didn't.

"No matter how we started a game, no matter how far we got behind, we always knew we had a chance with Doug," tight end Jimmie Giles once said.

Williams, whose final season salary of $120,000 ranked 54th among league quarterbacks, asked for a new five-year deal that would pay him $600,000 per year. Culverhouse would go no higher than $400,000.

"I think he would have been the perfect slave owner," Williams wrote in his 1990 autobiography *Quarterblack*. "Culverhouse thought I was a good ol' black boy who never had nothin' and would go along with whatever Mr. Culverhouse wanted. He paid me like his slave. My honest impression of Hugh Culverhouse is pretty much the same as anyone who knows him. If somebody wanted a perfect redneck asshole, Culverhouse would be a top candidate. He looked at his players as pieces of meat. We all knew what kind of person we were dealing with."

So, when the USFL came calling in 1983, Williams answered. He got his $600,000 from the Oklahoma Outlaws.

When the league folded in 1986, Williams signed with the Redskins. He didn't start that season. Actually, he threw only one pass.

But Williams threw a bunch during the 1987 season, including four that went for touchdowns in the second quarter alone of the Redskins' 42-10 wipeout of Denver in Super Bowl XXII in San Diego. It was there, earlier in the week, that Williams showed grace and tolerance amid the circus atmosphere that surrounded the first African-American quarterback to start a Super Bowl. By now, the question is the stuff of legend.

"Doug, how long have you been a black quarterback?"

Five days later, he was Super Bowl MVP, surrounded by cameras and microphones, headed for Disneyland.

Culverhouse, meanwhile, was back in Tampa.

"Hell, yeah, I was thinking about that. But I wasn't consumed," Williams said. "It'll eat you up if you make it about revenge. But when it's over, it hits you. You think about what you went through and what made you stronger. None of that matters, because you just did something nobody is ever going to take away. Like they say with the Bible, 'It is written.'"

And forever shall be.

"Letting Doug Williams walk away was the epitome of my father's overwhelming cheapness," Hugh Culverhouse Jr. said years after his father's death.

Williams retired from the NFL in 1990, opting for a coaching career that took him to his alma maters in high school (in Zachary, Louisana) and college. In February 2004, Williams left Grambling, where he won three Southwestern Athletic Conference titles, and returned to the Bucs as a personnel executive.

Twenty-one years later, Williams was back at One Buc Place. After all those years of reading defenses and calling plays from the sidelines, Williams was ready to take the game on from a booth high above the field.

"I'm going to get out of Jon Gruden's way," he said. "I don't want him turning to me and saying, 'Who the hell brought that guy in?'"

A more appropriate question: "Who the hell let that guy leave?"

Doug Williams You're Not

Well into the summer of '83, it became clear that Williams was departing.

"We had to do something," McKay said. "We simply couldn't wait any longer."

So Tampa Bay traded a first-round draft choice to Cincinnati for Jack Thompson, a young but heralded backup. Thompson played sparingly after being the third overall choice in the 1979 draft out of Washington State, where he left as the NCAA career record-holder in yards.

The Bucs were coming off their third postseason berth in four seasons. McKay figured the risk of trading such a high pick was worth it, given the playoff-ready state of his team.

"I like Doug, but I guess he has made a decision," McKay said. "We can't stand by and see time and our season slip by. We've already lost time."

Enter "The Throwin' Samoan."

"People will judge me by what I do, not what I say, and that is all you can ask for," Thompson said.

How true.

Thompson was beaten out in training camp by Jerry Golsteyn, who guided the Bucs through an unbeaten exhibition schedule. Golsteyn started the 1983 opener at home against Detroit.

The Bucs lost 11-0.

Thompson started in Week 3. He lost, and kept losing. Minus Williams, the Bucs dropped their first nine games, and the fans let Thompson have it. Thompson's numbers weren't awful (a team-record 58.9 percent completions, 2,906 yards, 18 TDs, 21 interceptions), but his poor decisions and turnovers came at the worst times.

"I owe somebody an apology. My teammates, coaches, Tampa," a beaten-down Thompson said following a midseason come-from-ahead loss courtesy of a late interception and touchdown return. "Until I can overcome mistakes like that, I won't be able to help this team."

He never overcame, never helped the team, and never was forgiven for not being Doug Williams.

"He is a nice young man who is maybe too sensitive," McKay said. "He was forewarned. The great Doug Williams fans who have been here all the years certainly are not Jack Thompson fans."

Tampa Bay finished the 1983 season 2-14. It was the worst record in the NFL, giving the Bucs the first overall choice in the 1984 draft.

Unfortunately, they'd already traded the pick.

For Thompson.

Frustration Was His Expertise

Imagine being a finalist for the male lead in *MacBeth*—against Anthony Hopkins.

Which brings us to Steve DeBerg's career.

"I'm usually competing with some kid they're calling the next Joe Namath," DeBerg said in 1987. Vinny Testaverde, the Heisman Trophy winner from Miami and No. 1 pick in the draft, was across the locker room at the time.

DeBerg's penance-like career saw him evolve into a solid, productive NFL quarterback, only to be confronted by potential greatness at training camps.

Even in Tampa.

At San Francisco, DeBerg started for almost three seasons for Bill Walsh before Joe Montana took over. DeBerg was traded to Denver in 1981, two years before the Broncos acquired John Elway.

In 1984, following the Bucs' disastrous experiment with Thompson, DeBerg was shipped to Tampa Bay for two draft picks. The results, both short and long term, were par for DeBerg's course.

DeBerg had command of the offense. Aided by running back James Wilder's breakout season, DeBerg completed 60.5 percent of his throws for 3,554 yards, 19 touchdowns and 18 interceptions. Unfortunately, Tampa Bay went 6-10 (with seven losses by seven points or less). The offense finished 10th overall in the NFL, still tied for the best ranking in team history.

The following September, Steve Young, a USFL refugee, wound up in Tampa with a $6 million contract.

"Here we go again," said DeBerg, who started the first 11 games.

The Bucs lost 10 of them.

Eventually, it was time to take a look at Young, the rookie.

"I totally understood," DeBerg said.

He always said that.

DeBerg won the starting job over Young at their second training camp, too. The opener was against his former team, the Niners, at home. The Bucs lost 31-7. DeBerg threw seven interceptions.

Said DeBerg: "I was terrible." So were the Bucs that year. Again. Young eventually took over the No. 1 job, but they still finished 2-14. Again.

By the time the 1987 season rolled around, Young had been traded to San Francisco and the Bucs had drafted Testaverde, who looked sensational in the preseason.

But DeBerg started the opener and threw five touchdowns in a 48-10 annihilation of Atlanta. His stats the rest of the season—good enough for an 85.3 passer rating—were winning numbers; only the Bucs didn't win. They lost their last eight, with Testaverde taking over for the stretch.

The next year DeBerg was traded to Kansas City. No Namaths awaited. No glory did, either.

"Just good enough to get you beat," was how Walsh once described DeBerg.

Likeable, personable and usually productive, DeBerg dealt with his Buccaneer Bermuda Triangle sentence like a pro.

"Sometimes, coaches get caught up in things just like fans and everybody else," DeBerg said. "There's a lot of mystique about a No. 1 draft choice quarterback. Now, add a Heisman Trophy, add a million-dollar baby and, all of a sudden, there's so much anticipation—"The Great Hope"—that they just can't wait; and it gets frustrating to have to wait."

Discarding a Future Hall of Famer

Young's legacy with the Bucs was defined by a game played in one of the worst blizzards in NFL history. Only 19,856 showed up at Lambeau Field in Green Bay on December 1, 1985.

The Bucs lost. The score was 21-0. The playing conditions were abominable.

Steve Young became a Hall of Fame-level player in San Francisco. In Tampa Bay, however, he was miscast as a dropback passer during his two seasons as a Buc. (The Tampa Tribune)

Sort of like the team's eventual discarding of Young, a future Hall of Famer.

"I look back on those days and in many ways I live in denial," Young said as he prepared to lead the 49ers to a 49-26 blowout of the Chargers in a six-touchdown, MVP performance at Super Bowl XXIX. "But I think any tough situation you're ever in, you learn and you grow from it."

Young starred at the university founded by and named for his great-great grandfather, Brigham Young, and became a high profile signing during the upstart USFL's raid on college players. He played two seasons for the Los Angeles Express, who signed Young to a 40-year, $43 million contract.

The Express, like most USFL teams, were in dire financial straits. The NFL recognized it and held a supplemental draft to prevent chaos in the event of mass defections. The Bucs, with the first overall pick by virtue of their league-worst record, took Young.

A little more than a year later, he bought out of his USFL deal and signed with the Bucs. Young joined the team a week into the season and rode the bench for 11 weeks.

With the Bucs 1-10, Young got his first start. Tampa Bay beat Detroit 19-16 in overtime, with Young marching the offense to the game-winning field goal.

The following week, the Bucs landed in Green Bay a few hours ahead of one of the worst blizzards to hit Wisconsin in years. The images of Young, clad completely in white, scrambling for his life in a foot of snow—facemask buried into the calf-deep powder of a real-life "Frozen Tundra"—were so pronounced that the people at Alka-Seltzer got permission from NFL Films to use the footage in a commercial for their cold medicine.

At the time, it was the only national television exposure the Bucs got.

And deserved.

In two seasons with Tampa Bay, Young experienced only four victories. As a starter he went 3-16, completing just over 50 percent of his passes and throwing nearly twice as many interceptions as touchdowns. Coach Leeman Bennett, 4-28 in two seasons, was fired. Ray Perkins, armed with the first overall pick in the draft, was hired.

One of Perkins's first acts was to post a list of his new players' optimum weights. He called a team meeting to explain how they'd be fined for not meeting his requirements. As his teammates got their first taste of Perkins's control freak ways, Young raised his hand and explained that he played better at a different weight than the coach had designated. Young asked if he could change his weight.

The word "no" was somewhere in the coach's profanity-laced answer.

"Ray Perkins used every word in the book," recalled linebacker Scot Brantley. "He totally embarrassed [Young] in front of the entire team, just shamed him to no end. I just said, 'Oh my God. Steve's got to get out of here.'"

Several months later, after the Bucs signed Testaverde to a lucrative contract before the draft, Young was traded to San Francisco for second- and fourth-round draft choices. At the time, the move was not second-guessed. The draft picks were used for linebacker Winston Moss and wide receiver Bruce Hill.

Young, free from what Walsh referred to as "an archaic offense," became one of the greatest quarterbacks in NFL history.

For the Bucs, the hits kept coming. And going.

The "Can't-Miss" That Did

The night before Testaverde signed a six-year, $8.2 million contract to join the Bucs in April 1987, media gathered at Tampa International Airport to greet the Heisman Trophy winner from Miami. The draft was three weeks away, and the Bucs had the first pick for the second straight year and appeared poised—at last—to end their run of rookie bad luck (See Jackson, Bo).

With reporters and TV cameras waiting, Testaverde was the first passenger to come through the gate.

"It's great to be here," he beamed before holding up a small, spherical object. "But, sorry, I've decided to play baseball."

It was a cruel joke.

Sort of like Testaverde's time in Tampa.

Six-foot-five, 220 pounds, strong, mobile and fast. Testaverde was the prototype when prototypes were all the rage. His contract was second only to Dan Marino's, and few questioned the payout. Across the league, the consensus was the Bucs had landed a franchise quarterback who would define the club.

In the Tampa Bay way, he did.

In his first start, Testaverde passed for a league single-game rookie-record 369 yards and two touchdowns at New Orleans. Tampa Bay lost 44-34, but as far as Bucs fans were concerned it was only a matter of time before headlines would scream, "VINNY, VIDI, VICI!"

"They have to understand, it's not going to happen overnight," Testaverde said. "There will be some games where it will be horrible, like a nightmare. Every game won't be like that one. But this is just a start. It will only get better."

Testaverde won the starting job outright heading into the 1988 season, which began at home against Philadelphia.

The Bucs trailed 34-0 at halftime.

Testaverde threw five interceptions in the 41-14 rout. He finished the season with 35 interceptions, the second most in NFL history, versus 13 touchdowns, as the team went 5-11.

Along the way, it was revealed that Testaverde suffered from a visual malady that made the Bucs' particular shade of orange appear white-ish—as in the opponent's uniform. Great. A colorblind, $8 million quarterback.

In his six seasons in Tampa Bay, Testaverde shattered nearly every passing record in the team's book—including interceptions. He threw 117 of them, compared to 77 touchdowns.

If the early and middle stages of his Bucs career were marred by inconsistency and disappointment, the latter part was defined by controversy. Several months following Perkins's firing, Testaverde called his former coach's offense "the most conservative in history." Perkins had a rebuttal.

"I just wish that No. 14 had a little more class," he said. "He has a big problem accepting blame. If he can go the other way, he'll have a better chance of becoming a great quarterback—and I have my doubts whether he ever will. He's an excuse-maker."

Testaverde also had issues with backup quarterback Chris Chandler during the one-year reign of Coach Richard Williamson, who in 1991 played Ping-Pong with the duo during a miserable 3-13 season. Chandler not only questioned Testaverde's heart and character ("I know I'll play harder for them than he will. I know I'll get up more times than he will."), but openly ripped his performance on the field.

"There's one guy who can go out and be totally inept and keep getting chances to have things go their way," Chandler said.

In 1993, Testaverde ended his association with the Bucs, signing a free-agent deal to join the Cleveland Browns as a backup to Bernie Kosar.

Another savior without a save.

"He's been loyal to this team," Coach Sam Wyche said at the time. "Whether Vinny was successful is a matter of opinion."

Unless, of course, statistics and won-loss records come into play.

Whipping Boy

The Bucs did not expect Trent Dilfer to be available when they picked sixth in the 1994 draft. Dilfer had led the nation in passing as a senior at Fresno State, capping his career with a 523-yard performance against Colorado in the Aloha Bowl. Another franchise quarterback. Another savior.

Save it.

Two years into his career, Dilfer had thrown five touchdowns and 24 interceptions and had become a poor fit in the locker room. Unlike the quarterbacks he competed against—Craig Erickson and Casey Weldon—Dilfer wasn't one of the guys. Erickson and Weldon brought their lunch pails to work, then threw a few back with the linemen afterward. Dilfer was married, a born-again Christian, honest and emotional to a fault.

Example: In an interview with *Sports Illustrated*, Dilfer recalled an NFL Films tribute to Montana in which a 49ers teammate expressed how much they loved their quarterback. Dilfer's eyes welled up as he told the writer how much he wanted to be loved by his teammates. "I want that kind of respect and affection so bad that I try to make it happen, and you can't do that. Joe never talked about it. It just happened."

Yet, one of Dilfer's more revealing moments came in the summer of 1996 when he and Weldon, friends by all accounts, got in a fight—an actual brawl—during a round of golf at a posh country club. While it might have been out of character, some of Dilfer's teammates saw it as a good sign.

The best sign of all, however, came in 1997 when Dilfer began projecting to expectations. He threw for more than 2,500 yards, 21 touchdowns and just 11 interceptions during Tampa Bay's surprising ascension to the playoffs. His numbers were nearly identical in '98, when the Bucs were eliminated from postseason contention the final week.

There was a sense that Dilfer, then 27 and coming into his own, might be the one.

"My ultimate goal is to be the only one who stayed here his whole career, the only quarterback who took the Tampa Bay Buccaneers to the Super Bowl," Dilfer said heading into 1999. "I only have control over me. And I've made it clear to fans, to media, to coaches, to management that I want to play another 10 years and to win multiple Super Bowls. Is this going to happen? I don't know."

It did and it didn't.

It did for Dilfer. Didn't for the Bucs.

Sound familiar?

Dilfer's season was a hybrid of his career. It started with his worst performance of all. With Dilfer accounting for four turnovers, two going for touchdowns, the Bucs lost 17-13 at home in their opener to the Giants, who became the first NFL team since 1960 to win a game with four first downs. The home crowd wanted blood. Dilfer sensed the locker room felt the same.

"It's difficult to look those guys in the eye, knowing I let not only the defense down, but all my teammates," he said. "I've got 15 games to make up for one bad one."

It took half the season and one benching before Dilfer found his rhythm. Unfortunately, it coincided with a broken collarbone at Seattle that ended his season, and, as it turned out, his Tampa Bay career.

The Bucs advanced to the NFC title game with rookie Shaun King in relief, choosing not to re-sign Dilfer. He signed with Baltimore, setting up one of the most surreal moments in Tampa Bay history.

Ten months later, Dilfer was headed back to Tampa to play in Super Bowl XXXV.

"Want me to set the scene in Tampa?" Ravens wide receiver Qadry Ismail said within Dilfer's earshot following Baltimore's 16-3 upset victory at Oakland in the AFC Championship Game. "OK, here goes. 'Oh, Trent, we love you. We were robbed. We want you back. Oh, Trent, you're the greatest.' I do believe we're about to get a lesson in 20-20 hindsight."

The defense-led Ravens demolished the Giants 34-7 to claim the club's first world championship. The rout began when Dilfer threw a 38-yard touchdown pass. Inserted at midseason for an ineffective Tony Banks, Dilfer went 11-0 as a starter.

"We all know I'm not Joe Montana," Dilfer said afterward. "But for the rest of my life I'm going to have this."

And if Bucs fans didn't know it, next-day headlines— "REDEMPTION!" screamed *The Tampa Tribune*, with a photo of Dilfer, both hands raised skyward—and quotes reminded them.

"Thank you, Tampa Bay. Thank you," Ravens tight end Shannon Sharpe said. "We appreciate it, y'all. You know, I think we'll keep him."

A month later, Dilfer was released.

It Was Good to Be King

The NFL's 1999 rookie class featured five quarterbacks drafted in the first 12 selections. Tim Couch, Donovan McNabb and Akili Smith went 1-2-3 overall, with Daunte Culpepper and Cade McNown called 11th and 12th, respectively.

King went 50th—then nearly went to the Super Bowl.

King, who grew up a Bucs fan in St. Petersburg, shattered the NCAA mark for passing efficiency while leading historically bad Tulane to a 12-0 record.

Eleven months later, King was in the unimaginable position of taking over as a rookie quarterback for a team in a championship run.

"It's just football, man," the 22-year-old King said over and over. "That's all."

He started the season as No. 3. Injuries changed that. With a defense playing spectacularly, King filled the role of caretaker. He threw a touchdown pass in relief against the Seahawks. He won his starting debut (on Monday night, no less) the following week against Minnesota. He threw for 297 yards and two touchdowns against Detroit his third time out, rallying the Bucs to victory with two touchdowns in the fourth quarter against a Lions defense that mocked the rookie.

"Some quarterbacks talk, but I'm not one of them. We'll look at the scoreboard after the game and see who's laughing," said King, an instant fan favorite. "The team feeds off the quarterback. If you get rattled, they get rattled. If you stay cool and composed, they do the same thing."

By the time Tampa Bay clinched his first division crown in 18 years, "Smoothie" King had completed 61 percent of his passes for 875 yards, seven touchdowns and four interceptions.

The rookie wasn't particularly sharp in Tampa Bay's playoff victory against Washington, but his game-winning touchdown pass made King the second rookie quarterback (the first since Los Angeles Ram Pat Haden in 1976) to start and win a playoff game.

A week later, King was under center in the NFC Championship Game at St. Louis, where the Bucs failed to score a touchdown in that heartbreaking 11-6 defeat.

A year later, the job all his own, King had some moments, but the Bucs—despite the arrival of wideout Keyshawn

Johnson—were shackled by a 26th-ranked passing game. The season ended with another touchdown-less playoff performance in a 21-3 loss at Philadelphia.

Two months after the season ended, the Bucs signed free agent Brad Johnson away from Washington with a six-year, $28 million deal. Just like that, King was a backup.

"I don't think anything worth having is ever easy," King said, reacting to the move. "I haven't complained. I haven't been bitter. OK, so there's a big obstacle I have to overcome."

King started one game (a loss) over the next three seasons, eventually bolting the team for a free-agent deal in Arizona in 2004. But the local-boy-makes-good angle was a nice story.

The Bull

Brad Johnson earned his nickname, "The Bull," through an uncompromising (and borderline warped) work ethic ingrained while growing up in Black Mountain, N.C.

Take the time in second grade when Ellen Johnson gave her physical education class a choice: either run five laps around the soccer field or jog the trail through the woods. The soccer field was longer, more tedious. The trail was easier, more fun. Every kid in the class chose the trail, except for one.

"No," she told eight-year-old Brad. "Everybody will be done and back in class before you run five times round that field."

"You gave us two choices," he barked back. "I'm running the field."

The son was relentless, the mom relented. Ellen walked off with her class, shaking her head, leaving Brad behind.

He was waiting for them in the classroom when they got back.

"I was right, and I knew it," Johnson recalled. "And I was going to prove it, too."

That sort of determination has kept Johnson in the NFL for 13 seasons. As a kid, he'd set goals of making 100 bull's-eyes and 300 50-pointers in darts before going to bed. Throw a football through a tire 20 straight times or else run. Take off on a sprint for every missed free throw.

Pressured discipline was his way of maintaining an edge.

"And I never changed," said Johnson, who rose from ninth-round draft pick and starter in Minnesota to reaching the Pro Bowl with the Redskins in 1999. He signed with Tampa Bay as a free agent in 2001.

He still arrives at quarterback meetings with a briefcase in tow. On Sundays, he demands a second uniform to change into at halftime, and clean socks after each quarter. As much as being obsessed by detail, Johnson is about maintaining a year-round routine.

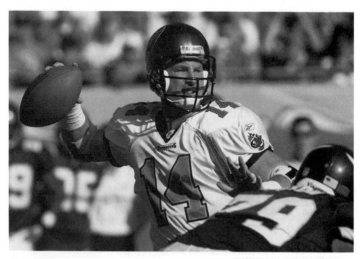

Brad Johnson drops to throw against the Vikings in 2002. Johnson, the NFC's leading passer that year, led the Bucs to the Super Bowl and also made the Pro Bowl. (The Tampa Tribune)

He claims to have done his own study over the years of how quarterbacks who put their feet up on the table or eat in meetings perform the following week versus those who don't.

"It all carries over, believe me," Johnson said.

In Gruden's first season, these meticulous traits translated into Pro Bowl numbers. After a pedestrian first year under Dungy, Johnson enjoyed a career season during Tampa Bay's run to the Super Bowl. He finished 2002 as the NFC top-rated passer, setting franchise records for completion percentage (62.3), touchdowns (22) and lowest interception percentage (1.3).

The Bucs, having grown accustomed to mediocrity (or worse) at football's most pivotal position, saw what can happen with a solid decision-maker and respected leader under center.

"He doesn't show it on the surface, but Brad's got an arrogance about him that he keeps to himself," receiver Joe Jurevicius said. "That's why he's such a good quarterback."

In Johnson's last six regular-season starts he threw 15 touchdowns and was picked off only once. In the postseason, he was intercepted once in the first quarter of each playoff game, then played near flawlessly thereafter. He fired a pair of touchdowns passes against the Raiders in the Super Bowl.

Not prone to emotional outbursts, Johnson broke into a mini-jig and Super Bowl chant, calling the fans to join in, as he stood at a podium in downtown Tampa following the team's world championship parade.

"Who was that guy?" General Manager Rich McKay wondered.

It was the same guy who attended a card-signing show in Atlantic City, New Jersey, a month later. Not exactly the headline act on the billboard, Johnson found himself surrounded by Magic Johnson, Emmitt Smith, Ronnie Lott and Marcus Allen. Each of them approached the quarterback.

"You know what they say?" Johnson asked. "They say, 'Congratulations, Champ!' And it sounds great."

Chapter 10

FROM THE BIZARRE

Me-Shawn

"If you have a problem with Keyshawn Johnson, you have a problem with yourself."

Who in the world would say such a thing?

Keyshawn Johnson.

At the Super Bowl, no less.

Two days later, on his Web site, he announced the end of his public statements.

"You can write the headline now: 'Keyshawn Not Talking To The Media For The Next Three Years,'" he wrote.

In less than 48 hours, after the Bucs won Super Bowl XXXVII, he was jabbering away and mugging for photographs.

What a trip.

Beyond the many receptions and too-few touchdowns, beneath the con-artist persona and shameless self-promotion, Keyshawn became much more than a football player. He was a walking, talking soap opera.

The Bucs grabbed Keyshawn, trading a pair of first-round picks to the New York Jets before the 2000 season. Naturally, there he was on the cover of *Sports Illustrated*, clutching a sword, wearing an eye-patch and bandana, and sneering at a headline: "The Almighty Buc."

His baggage was audacious. Keyshawn, the draft's overall No. 1 pick in 1996, wrote a book entitled, *Just Give Me The Damn Ball*. He was forever branded as self-absorbed and ego-driven. Detractors gave him a nickname: Me-Shawn.

Few people disputed his talent, especially his blocking and courage going across the middle. He made the Pro Bowl in 2001 by catching 106 passes. "Yeah, on hitches," Warren Sapp said. "Where we goin' with that?"

Not to the end zone—Keyshawn had just one touchdown—especially when his old team, the Jets, came to Tampa in 2000.

The Keyshawn Bowl

Prior to Jets-Bucs in 2000, Keyshawn scolded Tampa Bay media for "creating a story" and "wanting a soap opera." But Keyshawn created his own controversy by slamming Jets receiver Wayne Chrebet, his former teammate.

"You're trying to compare a flashlight to a star," Keyshawn told a New York reporter when asked about his relationship with Chrebet. "Flashlights only last so long. A star is in the sky forever." To boot, Keyshawn said he wouldn't shake hands with Jets coach Al Groh, whom he blamed for not getting a renegotiated contract.

On the practice field, incensed at being shadowed by a CNN cameraman, he extended his middle finger and glared into the lens.

He was reprimanded. He apologized. But all along, Keyshawn knew what he was doing. He held three news conferences during the week. He was the show.

For the Bucs, the game couldn't have unfolded in worse fashion.

On a water-logged afternoon, Keyshawn had just one reception (on a shovel pass, at that) for one yard. The Bucs clung to a three-point lead with 1:39 remaining. Mike Alstott, trying to run out the clock, lost a fumble at the Tampa Bay 24-yard line, giving the Jets a final chance.

Cue the movie script. Jets running back Curtis Martin got the pitch, swept right, then rose up for a wobbly option pass to the end zone.

It was caught for an 18-yard touchdown.

By Wayne Chrebet.

Afterward, Groh couldn't resist a jab at Keyshawn. "I guess the power of a flashlight can be pretty bright sometimes," he said.

The Jets had scored 15 points in the space of one minute to beat the Bucs, 21-17.

As for Keyshawn—one catch for one yard?

"I can't explain it," he said. "How can I explain it? I just don't think they (Bucs coaches) understand the type of football player I am yet."

Keyshawn's foil had the last laugh. Some Bucs, looking at the bigger picture, began to seethe about the attention afforded to Keyshawn.

"I don't give a damn about Keyshawn," Bucs guard Frank Middleton said. "I don't give a damn if he had 20 catches or no catches. This was about the Bucs trying to get to 4-0, not about Keyshawn putting on a show."

The show had just begun.

It even had a surprise ending. Ten games into the 2003 season, coach Jon Gruden finally tired of Keyshawn's act. The receiver was deactivated and paid not to play for the Bucs. Could it have finished any other way?

Here's the Kicker

Coach John McKay once said of place-kickers: "They are like grass. They are everywhere."

The Bucs had them in all shapes, sizes and temperaments. Just before the inaugural exhibition game, kicker Booth Lusteg announced he wouldn't dress for the game unless he had white shoes. Assistant equipment manager Frankie Pupello bought some white paint, which he neatly applied to Lusteg's black shoes. It didn't help. Lusteg soon was released.

Neil O'Donoghue, a six foot six Irishman whose short field goal in 1979 gave Tampa Bay its first playoff berth, was best known for a play that still can be seen on *Football Follies* highlights. At Minnesota, after a sailed center snap, O'Donoghue gave chase. Perhaps relying on his soccer background, O'Donoghue tried to boot the ball, but whiffed and crumbled to the turf. The ball was scooped by a Viking who returned it to the Tampa Bay 10-yard line (making it an 80-yard loss from the original line of scrimmage).

Steve Christie displayed Pro Bowl form in 1990 and '91. Sam Wyche, who became head coach in 1992, placed Christie on a list of unprotected players because the kicker assured him he wasn't going anywhere. Christie promptly signed with the Buffalo Bills and played in two Super Bowls.

Tampa Bay's best-performing kicker, Martin Gramatica, was unrestrained in his jubilant emotions after nearly every kick, whether it was a game-winning 50-yarder, a chip-shot or an extra point. *Tampa Tribune* photographer David Kadlubowski won an award for capturing the high-jumping, screaming Gramatica—after he made a first-half field goal during an exhibition game.

Getting the Boot

Bill Capece put the Bucs into the 1982 playoffs with last-minute field goals against Detroit and Chicago.

But he's best remembered for three little words.

"Capece is kaput."

McKay's parting shot.

In 1983, Capece missed three extra points and converted only 10 of 23 field-goal attempts. The capper was a 12-9 overtime loss to the Packers on *Monday Night Football.* Capece shanked an extra point that would have won the game in regulation, then plunked a 35-yard field-goal attempt in overtime.

"I lost the football game by being stupid enough to think that we could kick a field goal," McKay said. "We will not kick a field goal next week if we are on the 2-yard line, the 1-yard line, none. There will be no more kicked field goals by the Bucs this year, no matter what the score is, no matter what the game is.

"It's over. I'm tired of being crucified by all these wonderful Florida people. God bless you and Merry Christmas."

The story gets better (or worse, if you're Capece).

The Bucs immediately signed free agent Dave Warnke, who watched Capece's performance and cold-called a Tampa Bay scout to ask for a shot. Warnke kicked a 53-yard field goal while McKay was watching (ironically, shortly after Capece left practice with a pulled groin muscle). Capece later said his inconsistency began with bad center snaps and the changing of his holder.

McKay read those words.

Uh-oh.

In the season finale at Detroit, McKay initially was true to his vow. With the game scoreless, the Bucs went for it on fourth and inches at the Detroit 11-yard line, but were repelled.

Later, Warnke was summoned for a 29-yard field-goal attempt. He missed badly. When the Bucs scored a touchdown, Warnke's extra-point attempt also missed badly. He was done.

McKay disdained another field-goal try, but the Bucs came up short on fourth down at the Detroit 5. All told, it was seven potentially wasted points in a game won by Detroit 23-20.

The Bucs scored a late touchdown, and McKay sent in offensive lineman George Yarno for the PAT. His left-footed

Bucs coach John McKay with kicker Bill Capece during practice in 1983. Capece will forever be remembered for McKay's quip: "Capece is kaput." (The Tampa Tribune)

boot split the uprights. CBS cut to a shot of McKay, who couldn't resist a smirk.

"It just proves what Bill Capece and others say," McKay said. "We have a professional holder and a professional snapper. Now all we need to find is a professional kicker. It just took a professional kicker to do it. Unfortunately, he turned out to be a lineman."

The upshot?

"Capece is kaput."

After retiring (and perhaps with a final nod to Capece), McKay said, "My whole career here was a missed extra point."

The Unkindest Cut of All

Free agent wide receiver Alvin Harper, signed in 1995, suffered a series of injuries and was surly to boot.

Midway through his second and final season in Tampa Bay, the tip of Harper's left middle finger was accidentally sliced by trainer Joe-Joe Petrone. By then, his absence in the lineup was hardly missed. Appearing in the 1996 regular-season finale against Chicago, Harper received a mock standing ovation after catching a pass. Pressed about his future, Harper told reporters, "I'm not entertaining you all today. Get out of my damn face."

Harper was released by Tampa Bay and signed by Washington. It figured that the Redskins would open the 1997 exhibition season at Tampa Bay. It also figured that Harper would catch a 60-yard touchdown pass against his old team. After crossing the goal line, Harper angrily punted the ball into the end-zone cheap seats.

He Could Go All the Way? Nah

Through their first 28 seasons, the Bucs never returned a kick-off for a touchdown. Not one. That was 1,645 consecutive returns (not including touchbacks or kicks that were downed in the end zone).

To put that in perspective, the expansion New Orleans Saints in 1967 needed just one chance. John Gilliam returned the first kickoff in team history for a touchdown.

Strangely, Tampa Bay's Isaac Hagins scored on two kickoff returns during the initial 1976 exhibition season, but they didn't count. On the first play of Gruden's coaching tenure in Tampa Bay, Frank Murphy returned the opening kickoff for a touchdown in an exhibition against Miami. That didn't count either.

"It's hard to believe," former Tampa Bay return man Karl Williams once said. "Maybe they should put it on *Unsolved Mysteries* or something."

"Whoever gets that first touchdown will go down in Tampa Bay history," Aaron Stecker said.

In 2001, Stecker almost became the man. On the opening kickoff against New Orleans—the 1,538th return in franchise history—he bulled through three would-be tacklers and raced for 86 yards before being tripped up by the ankles.

Since 1999, Budweiser had periodically sponsored the "Million-Dollar Runback." A selected fan could watch the game from the sideline. And if the Bucs returned a kickoff for a touchdown, that fan would win $1 million.

Heading into the 2004 season, it remained the safest giveaway promotion in sports.

Cheapskates

When the Bucs made Super Bowl XXXVII, the Glazers flew all their employees to San Diego for the week. It was a spare-no-expense gesture—and quite a departure from the bygone era.

Hugh Culverhouse once told his chief assistant, Phil Krueger, "Don't become friends with my money." Penny pinching reached ridiculous proportions.

After a road trip, one Bucs official noticed a local phone call (75 cents) had been made from a room shared by two players. The offending party couldn't be identified. So both players had 38 cents deducted from their next paycheck. The Bucs made a penny on the deal.

In 1985, Bucs safety David Greenwood made his first NFL interception and wanted to keep the ball. Nope, said Krueger. "He wanted me to pay for it and said it would be 35 bucks," Greenwood said. "It wasn't worth it." The ball was returned.

Sunday Afternoon at the Fights

There weren't many fireworks in coach Ray Perkins's inaugural season of 1987, unless you count the locker room at halftime. The Bucs were trailing 28-10 at New Orleans, and offensive tackle Ron Heller tried to keep spirits up.

"Let's go, guys, don't quit," Heller said.

Perkins snapped and started punching Heller.

"I heard the word, 'Quit, let's don't quit,' and I just turned and attacked," said Perkins, who broke a ring and pinky finger after slamming into the helmet of Heller, who outweighed him by 100 pounds. "I don't even like to hear the word. I'm not a quitter. It wasn't a fight."

Three years later, Heller begged to differ.

"He punched me in the mouth," Heller said while playing with the Philadelphia Eagles in 1990. "I kept pushing him away and said, 'Coach, you've got the wrong guy.' But he kept coming at me. That's when I got him by the throat and I was ready to lay him out. He came back at me again and I said, 'All right, blankety-blank-blank. You want to start. Let's go.' Then he walked away.

"I swear he had it premeditated. He was going to start something to try and get us fired up."

The Bucs lost 44-34.

One Buc Place

Nearly every NFL franchise operates in plush training facilities. The Bucs continue to use One Buc Place, an antiquated building so cramped that assistants have closet-sized offices, the weight room spills outdoors onto the back porch's heavy humidity, and many staff members work in trailers. It's an eyesore to be avoided for potential free agents. In executive offices, traps are set to catch the resident rats.

Gruden, who calls One Buc the "woodshed," was forced from his film-watching cave in 2003 when the building's main air-conditioning compressor exploded. "One Buc," Gruden said. "That's about all it's worth. One buck."

The Bucs' set-up has improved. Training camp once was held at One Buc, with players housed next door at the old Hall of Fame Inn. Former linebacker Scot Brantley said he once awakened to find a frog wrapped around his toothbrush. "To say it was on the decline would be doing decline an injustice," former GM Rich McKay said.

How things have changed. Since 2002, the Bucs have held training camp at Celebration, the Disney-styled Central Florida community that features the lap of luxury, including a 115-room luxury boutique resort that the Bucs reserve for a month.

Even the days at One Buc are numbered. In 2006, the Bucs expect to be in their new $30 million training facility, which could carry the name of a corporate sponsor.

Booker Reese and the Busts

The Bucs were coming off an NFC Central Division title. Personnel chief Ken Herock was enamored with defensive end Booker Reese, a six-foot-six raw-boned prospect from tiny Bethune-Cookman College. Reese wasn't a sure thing, but Herock and assistant coach Abe Gibron felt the player had star potential.

On draft day, the Bucs were picking 17th in the first round. The braintrust was divided between Reese's upside and the stability of Penn State guard Sean Farrell. Word was Farrell could be difficult to sign.

Equipment manager Pat Marcuccillo was at the Bucs' draft table in New York, sitting by a speaker phone. When the Bucs were on the clock, chaos ensued.

Marcuccillo was told to write "Sean Farrell, guard, Penn State" on a card. The speaker phone momentarily malfunctioned, and Marcuccillo didn't hear Herock's instructions to write "Booker Reese, defensive end, Bethune-Cookman" on another card. In the meantime, Farrell's agent painted a hard-line stance with the Bucs during a brief telephone conversation, swinging the pendulum toward Reese.

Holding the Farrell card, Marcuccillo noticed the Bucs only had a few minutes on the clock. "Should I turn it in?" he said.

The speaker phone crackled, with sound fading in and out. Herock's message was to select Reese, but the only thing

Marcuccillo heard was "… turn it in." So off went the Farrell card to the podium.

When Farrell's selection was announced in New York, a hush fell over the draft room at One Buc Place. The Bucs had taken the wrong player (at least in Herock's opinion). McKay, backing Herock's instincts, soon worked a trade with Chicago. The Bucs got an early second-round pick, which they used for Reese, and surrendered a 1983 first-rounder.

Reese never panned out. He wasn't a cornerstone, on or off the field.

When he signed, Reese took his bonus check, in excess of $100,000, and immediately headed to a car dealership to purchase a vehicle. He picked one out, then handed his check to the salesman, who replied, "What do you want to do with this?" Reese shrugged. "I guess give me the change."

Reese's rookie season was shredded by a 57-day player strike. Even that was a welcome reprieve. He complained of constant headaches early in training camp. One of his coaches at Bethune-Cookman, Cy McClairen, later said Reese had been issued an undersized helmet, but the player was too timid to complain.

Following two underachieving seasons, Reese was traded to the Los Angeles Rams for a 12th-round draft pick. With Tampa Bay, he played in 24 games, starting just seven. And the pick Tampa Bay surrendered for Reese's rights? Chicago used it for productive wide receiver Willie Gault.

Other personnel busts from the Buc Hall of Shame:

Tampa Bay acquired defensive end and former Pro Bowler Wally Chambers from Chicago, but he only played two seasons because of knee problems. The Bucs surrendered a first-round draft choice, which the Bears used for defensive lineman Dan Hampton, a Hall of Famer.

Tampa Bay gave up first-round draft choices for quarterbacks Jack Thompson (1983) and Chris Chandler (1990). Both lasted just two seasons and were cut, so the Bucs got nothing for them.

Tampa Bay used the fourth overall pick in the 1990 draft for Alabama linebacker Keith McCants, despite reports of knee problems, and he lasted only three seasons. The Bucs bypassed Junior Seau and Emmitt Smith, among others.

Other premium picks used for players that languished: Offensive tackle Charles McRae (seventh overall in 1991) and defensive end Eric Curry (sixth overall in 1993).

Farrell's Yuletide Cheer

Of course, it makes sense that Farrell (the player picked by accident) worked out fine with the Bucs. And it's perfectly logical that he said his unofficial goodbye to the franchise during a 1986 appearance before an Orlando booster club.

"I know what I want this Christmas—I want to get the hell out of Tampa Bay," Farrell said. "I don't care where I'm going. I just want out."

Hello and Goodbye

In 1978, Jimmy DuBose had the first 100-yard rushing game in Tampa Bay history. Just after breaking that barrier, DuBose attempted a tackle following an interception. He suffered severe ligament damage in his left knee and never played again.

In 1986, free-agent rookie Nathan Wonsley subbed for the injured James Wilder and rushed for 138 yards against the Lions. Later, he had a 108-yard performance—and a 59-yard touchdown run—against the Rams. But prior to a game against

Chicago, the Bucs needed someone for the kickoff coverage team. The ever gung-ho Wonsley answered the call. On the opening kickoff, Wonsley broke his neck in a collision with Bears returner Thomas Sanders. Outside of a brief comeback attempt in the 1989 exhibition season, Wonsley never played again.

The Unfriendly Skies

With Culverhouse trying to save cash, the 1976 team used a charter discount airline that had just two planes and was on the verge of bankruptcy. Some players were frightened, especially after traveling to the first regular-season game at Houston, when the plane had a rapid descent and practically crash-landed. Later in the season, because of the airline's financial woes, Tampa Bay's plane was not cleared for take-off following a road game. Culverhouse used a credit card to purchase fuel so the Bucs could return home.

The Agony of Victory

Detroit was at Tampa Bay for the 1988 regular-season finale. Both teams were 4-11. The winner would get the sixth overall draft selection, while the loser would claim the third overall pick.

The Bucs prevailed 21-10.

With the sixth pick, the Bucs selected Nebraska linebacker Broderick Thomas, who held out, started slowly and had a few nice moments with some bad teams.

With the third pick, the Lions selected Oklahoma State running back Barry Sanders, one of the NFL's all-time best talents who tormented the Bucs for a decade.

The enduring question: Which team really won?

The World's Longest Bathroom Break

During 1976 training camp, tight end Ricou deShaw, a free agent from Miami, asked coaches if he could take a bathroom break. Sure, he was told. DeShaw was seen sprinting off the field, headed for the locker room at One Buc Place.

DeShaw removed his helmet, jersey, football pants, cleats and pads. He cleaned out his locker. And he was never seen again.

The story was passed down through Buc generations. Ricou deShaw, the smartest man of all, the player who beat it before all the miserable defeats occurred.

If only it was true.

During the week of Super Bowl XXXVII, deShaw was located by *Tampa Tribune* columnist Martin Fennelly. DeShaw, who works for an engineering firm in the Florida Keys, said it was a fairy tale. He said he departed after injuring his back and outside doctors told him to quit playing.

With apologies to deShaw, should we let facts get in the way of a good story?

Going Nowhere

Tight end David Grannell was cut by Dallas in 1976, then claimed by Tampa Bay two days before the Bucs played their first exhibition game at Los Angeles.

Grannell, leaving the Cowboys' training camp in Thousand Oaks, California, flew all day on a Thursday to reach Tampa. The next day, he was on the Bucs' charter flight with new teammates and headed back to Southern California. Grannell, who didn't play in Tampa Bay's 26-3 loss to the Rams, flew back to Tampa on the team plane.

By Monday, Grannell was released.

He immediately booked a flight to his hometown.

In California.

The King of Preseason

In 1982, one season after he was a $500-per-year player for the semipro Orlando Americans, quarterback Jerry Golsteyn was signed by the Bucs. For two summers worth of exhibition games, Golsteyn was the greatest quarterback in Tampa Bay history. He completed 62.6 percent of his passes for 1,028 yards, eight touchdowns and no interceptions in eight practice games, giving him a preseason quarterback rating of 129.1.

Reluctantly, McKay named Golsteyn as his starter to open the 1983 season. The preseason flash was never seen again. Golsteyn managed just a 56.8 QB rating in the regular season, and failed to throw a touchdown pass. He was released before training camp in 1984.

"Jerry's a nice kid," McKay said. "But so is my wife. And she's no quarterback."

Order Up a Play

In a fund-raiser for the Leukemia Society of America, Bucs coach Sam Wyche allowed representatives from Outback Steakhouse and Hooters to call the team's first two plays in a 1992 exhibition game at Denver.

Outback: Vinny Testaverde hit tight end Ron Hall with a 26-yard completion after a play-action fake.

Hooters: Testaverde walked away from the huddle toward the sideline, in apparent confusion. A quick long snap went to running back Gary Anderson, who swept for 14 yards. Unfortunately, the gadget play was wiped out by a holding penalty.

Before the game, Broncos coach Dan Reeves told Wyche the plays better not go for touchdowns or else "those restaurants may be calling the plays all season."

Great Timing

When Perkins had his initial draft class in 1987, a Tampa Bay news release quoted him as saying the No. 1 pick, Testaverde, "should be a great quarterback. And I don't use the word 'great' too many times."

Excerpts from the same news release:

Perkins described cornerback Ricky Reynolds as having "the great speed."

Running back Don Smith was "a great competitor."

Linebacker Henry Rolling had "great movement."

Perkins was impressed with the "great hands" of wide receiver Bruce Hill.

Running back Steve Bartolo was "a great individual."

Vinny the Punching Bag

Gene Upshaw, executive director of the NFL Players Association, was forced to apologize to Testaverde following an embarrassing incident in 1988. Upshaw was being interviewed by Jim Gray on NBC's *NFL Live!* During a commercial break, Gray asked Upshaw about the quality of league quarterbacks, bringing up Testaverde.

"I'm better than Testaverde!" Upshaw said.

Upshaw added he heard Testaverde once was cutting hedges while dragging an electrical cord through a swimming pool.

Off-the-air chit-chat?

Actually, Upshaw's remarks were picked up on a clean nationwide feed by countless satellite-dish viewers. The incident made the newspapers and was reported on ESPN.

Upshaw called it "eavesdropping" and said the remarks were "just kidding around, total b.s. kind of stuff." But the damage had been done.

"I sure wouldn't say anything bad about a guy I represent," a contrite Upshaw said, after being confronted by an angry Perkins. "That would be plain stupid. That team has enough problems without this to worry about."

Hunting for Fans

At Green Bay, team president Gay Culverhouse was delighted to see thousands of fans wearing orange. She thought it was an unexpectedly large group of traveling Bucs fans. Then someone broke the news. "Uh, those are hunting jackets."

On the Radio

The Bucs once had a future Minnesota governor—or a wrestler-turned-actor, depending on your taste—as one of their radio network's color commentators. Jesse "The Body" Ventura graced Tampa Bay's airwaves for two seasons with a gravelly voice and observations that sometimes came out of left field.

"Doesn't Ray Perkins look like Al Bundy on *Married With Children?*" Ventura once mused during a Bucs' drive.

It might not have been award-winning radio, but the Bucs received a ton of publicity with several magazine articles and a feature on HBO's *Inside The NFL.*

Ventura's appearance was a subtle shift in philosophy from Tampa Bay's first play-by-play man, the legendary Ray Scott, who made his renowned reputation with a brevity of words on Green Bay broadcasts: "Starr ... Dowler ... touchdown."

With the winless Bucs, Scott's calls went more like, "Spurrier ... dropping ... sacked."

Ice Follies

Through the bad years, and even through most of the good ones, the Bucs had a constant nemesis when going on the road. They couldn't win in the cold. Their chances melted at the sight of snow. Annual NFC Central pilgrimages to Green Bay and Chicago were lost causes if the NFL schedule-maker placed them in November or December.

The Bucs had been 0-21 in temperatures below 40 degrees, until finally breaking through during the Super Bowl championship season of 2002. First, the Bucs ended the regular season drought with a win (temperature: 28 degrees) against the Bears in Champaign, Illinois. "It helped us because, once and for all, we didn't have to listen to that cold-weather thing anymore," Bucs general manager Rich McKay said.

The Bucs then defeated Philadelphia in the NFC Championship Game (temperature: 26 degrees).

Maybe the shiver-me-timbers legacy can be forgotten, but it can't be denied.

Assorted facts about Tampa Bay's performance in those 21 chilly losses:

The Bucs averaged 232.3 yards while surrendering 322.3.

They had a minus-17 turnover ratio.

They scored an average of 9.0 points, while allowing 24.3.

They led only twice in the fourth quarter.

Only one Bucs running back rushed for 100 yards in cold weather (William Howard, 101 against New England in 1988). Only one Bucs quarterback passed for 300 yards (Trent Dilfer, 312 against Green Bay in 1995).

Tampa Bay's ultimate cold-weather nightmare occurred on December 1, 1985. Tampa Bay at Green Bay. It's better known as the Snow Bowl.

There were 35,586 no-shows for the game at Lambeau Field. The Bucs were outgained 512 yards to 65 and lost 21-0. Bucs quarterback Steve Young was sacked into a snow bank and quickly popped up, arms flailing, unable to see or breathe.

Better days were ahead. These days, the Bucs refuse to acknowledge cold-weather excuses. They play in the NFC South, not the NFC Central. And just for the record, Gruden's teams are unbeaten in sub-40-degree games.

Chapter 11

THE BIG THREE

Putting the Pieces in Place

The 1995 NFL draft was one to savor. On the back porch of One Buc Place, General Manager Rich McKay and college scouting director Tim Ruskell wheeled out the video machine, opened a couple beers and fired up cigars.

They watched Warren Sapp's intimidating presence. They watched the sideline-to-sideline intensity of Derrick Brooks. They dreamed of what was to come.

"A lot of people had questions about Warren and Derrick," McKay said. "We did not. We felt they were the players we could build a defense around."

When Sapp showed up for his first mini-camp, he strolled into the weight room and saw strong safety John Lynch.

"So you're that bad-ass white boy I've been hearing about," Sapp said. "You ready to start winning?"

Lynch, two seasons into a career with a floundering franchise, nodded.

"Let's do it."

No one can pinpoint exactly when the Bucs began marching to the beat of Sapp, Brooks and Lynch. In a way, it seems like they were always there, making plays, barking instructions, motivating teammates.

Lynch, from an affluent family in Southern California, was an example of perfect decorum off the field. Between the lines, though, he hit like a torpedo. Sapp and Brooks came from Florida, but couldn't be more different. Sapp talked big and played bigger, using emotion and controversy as fuel. Brooks was a quiet worker, an example-setter.

Now, they were joining forces.

"We don't really hang out together off the field," Lynch said. "But we'll be forever linked."

The first lines of defense.

John Lynch—Class Act, Callous Farewell

On the Same Plane

Following a lopsided 1995 defeat, Lynch was trying to rest through a throbbing headache during a return flight to Tampa. From a few rows back, Sapp, the rookie, tossed a playing card, then another, at his teammate.

"Please stop, Warren," Lynch asked.

Another.

"Stop it," Lynch repeated.

The next one brought Lynch to his feet.

"If you don't cut it out, something's going down between us," he warned, before settling back into his seat.

Moments after the next—and last—card hit Lynch in the head, it took about a half-dozen teammates to restrain him.

Lynch's action took Sapp by surprise and brought about a realization.

"Oh yeah," he thought. "I can go to war with this guy."

Man for the People

During his 11 seasons, Tampa Bay players, civic leaders and fans learned that Lynch, a third-round draft pick from Stanford in 1993, could be counted on. Aside from co-captaining a defense that won a Super Bowl in his hometown of San Diego, Lynch took active roles in charitable organizations and scholarship foundations while voicing support for Tampa's military population.

"There's truly no chance John Lynch's name shows up in the Metro section of your newspaper, unless he's giving away money, presenting a scholarship or kissing a baby," McKay said. "Put it this way: As an ambassador for our franchise, not bad."

When Lynch received a six-year, $24 million contract extension at the start of the 2000 season he vowed to commit $1,000 per victory, $500 per interception or sack and $100 per tackle to his John Lynch Foundation, devoted to molding youth leaders in the community.

To think, he wondered early on if he'd made the right career choice. Lynch was a second-round draft choice by baseball's Florida Marlins, threw the first pitch in the organization's history and had a 2.14 ERA in one season of rookie league before Coach Sam Wyche called. Any doubts Lynch had were gone by the 1996 season when he cracked the starting lineup.

In the 1997 playoff victory against Detroit, Lynch set an early tone with the kind of devastating hit that became his trademark and helped him land five invitations to the Pro Bowl. Barry Sanders called the collision the hardest blow of his career.

"I've been waiting for a lick like that on that guy for a long time," Lynch said.

Strong safety John Lynch leaves the field happy after a win at Cincinnati in 2001. His John Lynch Foundation made several hundred Tampa youths happy as well. (The Tampa Tribune)

A message had been sent. The Bucs had a wrecking ball in the secondary.

"When they get off the bus, they're already looking for No. 47, believe me," defensive coordinator Monte Kiffin said.

Brotherly (In-Law) Love

In a 1997 game against Chicago, Lynch put a kill shot on Bears tight end John Allred. The hit was worth noting on two points. First, Lynch and Allred had been teammates and close friends at Stanford. Second, Lynch married Allred's sister, Linda.

As Allred was being helped off the field, Bucs defensive tackle Brad Culpepper had a message.

"Not only did he knock you out of the game, he's sleeping with your sister."

But more than a decade of bone-jarring hits took their toll. Lynch began suffering from painful stingers during the 2003 season, though he played through the agony. After the season, he had shoulder surgery to correct the problem. Little did he know that the most devastating blow of his career was on the horizon.

How Could They?

On March 10, 2004, new General Manager Bruce Allen, on the job barely two months, telephoned Lynch in California and told one of the franchise treasures that he no longer fit into its plans and that promising third-year pro Jermaine Phillips needed to play. Lynch, due to make more than $4 million in 2004, offered to take a pay cut, but was turned down.

Casting off Lynch like some journeyman was a dark day for an organization that had distanced itself from public-relations gaffes. There had to be a better way to cut ties with Lynch than a phone call from a front-office exec he barely knew.

"I don't agree with it," said Lynch, whose 973 tackles (third most in team history) suddenly meant nothing. "I think it's wrong."

On the most bitter day of his professional career, those were the harshest words that came from Lynch, whose farewell speech to Tampa Bay came from a radio station in San Diego. Just like that, he was gone.

"I thought I had an opportunity to spend my whole career in one spot, which is a tough thing to do. I guess I'm kind of an idealist," Lynch said. "I'll be playing somewhere else next year, but I'll always be a Buccaneer in my heart."

He signed with Denver.

Warren Sapp—Bad Enough for the Bull's-Eye

Attitude Adjustment

During the '90s, the Bucs held joint training camp workouts with the Miami Dolphins almost annually. The venue changed, but the tone of practices remained a constant.

The routine: Dolphins shoved Bucs from sideline to sideline, smashed their faces into the turf and walked away laughing. The Bucs took it.

Then they took Sapp in the draft.

Five years into Sapp's career, a rookie Dolphins tackle, Todd Wade, took exception to Sapp's gyrating and taunting ways during scrimmages. Wade verbalized a lack of respect for the reigning NFL Defensive Player of the Year with unflattering remarks that were taken back to Sapp for retort.

"Who?" Sapp asked. "Anybody got a number on him?"

That year, the Dolphins returned to South Florida, complaining of the Bucs arrogance. The mere notion of such a thing—repeat: Bucs arrogance—was once not only unfathomable, but laughable.

Defensive tackle Warren Sapp, a menacing presence on the field, created as much furor with his outlandish remarks as his play. (AP/WWP)

"When Warren got here, everything changed," McKay said. "He brought an attitude."

Mad at the World

In that memorable draft of 1995, the Bucs selected one of the most decorated Miami Hurricanes in history; a Category 5 in football pads, with a chip on his shoulder.

Sapp deserved to be one of the top four picks in the draft, but *The New York Times* took care of that. The paper reported Sapp tested positive for cocaine and marijuana at the NFL Combine more than a month earlier. The league answered the charge by releasing a statement saying the report of Sapp's failed cocaine test was inaccurate. The rebuttal mentioned nothing about pot, however.

On draft day, with each passing pick (and passing millions), Sapp grew more defiant. By the time the Bucs called his name at No. 12, a firestorm was bubbling inside. Sapp was in no mood to screw on a smile as he raised a Tampa Bay jersey alongside Commissioner Paul Tagliabue. All he could think about were the 11 teams that picked someone else.

"I hope they're all on the schedule," he said.

Sapp, in time, would exact his revenge in a bombastic and antagonistic manner that garnered attention but endeared him to few. The fact that he grew into one of the game's most feared players, though, made him matter.

Warren Sapp, superstar.

Warren Sapp, anti-hero.

It was perfect.

"It's hard to bend a man's words when they're as straight as mine are," Sapp said. "How you gonna bend steel?"

Indoctrination and Intimidation

That first year, Sapp's veteran teammates mocked him with the nickname "Super Rookie." To think that pedestrians such as Santana Dotson and Mark Wheeler dared engage Sapp seems curious, but then Sapp wasn't a great rookie. In his second year, the team's first under Tony Dungy, his development began. His nine sacks led the team.

In 1997, Sapp was at the forefront of the team's new fame. His facial expressions and sound bites played masterfully. The look was menacing, but engaging. He became a favorite of the national press.

Back in Tampa, however, it was love-hate. There was no questioning Sapp's devotion. He was always there, on time, and no one worked harder.

But Sapp was rude and confrontational to fans. Any stories of Sapp's warm side were lost amid accounts of brushoffs that were as regular as his brush-asides of offensive lineman. Sapp fed off the bully perception, though, and his image became a human blaze.

"They're not paying me at the grocery store to entertain them. That's my time," Sapp reasoned. "And if you're going to come up to somebody and ask them for their time, do it in a polite and courteous manner. ... I get demands all the time. I'm the head of my household. I give orders. I don't take them."

Among his greatest hits:

• The year after breaking Lee Roy Selmon's single-season sack record, Sapp dared to call out Mark Gastineau, convicted spouse-batterer and holder of the NFL mark. "I don't think a guy sitting on Rikers Island should have his name at the top of an NFL record book, and I'm going to take it down." When Sapp finished with just 6 1/2 sacks, he shrugged off his prediction. "When you shoot for the moon, sometimes you hit the stars."

• Heading into a game at New Orleans, Sapp was asked if he planned to spend time on Bourbon Street with Saints quarterback Kerry Collins, who was battling alcoholism. "My wife doesn't let me hang out with drunks."

• Giants defensive end Mike Strahan bested Gastineau's mark on the final week of the 2001 season. The record-setting sack, which came against Sapp's admired rival Brett Favre, raised eyebrows over the appearance that Favre surrendered it intentionally in the final minute. Sapp was the only one who dared say so. "Asterisk," Sapp declared prior to arriving at 2002 training camp. "If Derrick Thomas was alive, he'd have an asterisk on it. Reggie White has an asterisk on it. All the big boys who hunt have an asterisk on it." Told of Sapp's remarks, Strahan labeled Sapp a "jackass" who "wished he were me." He added, "Get out of the first round of the playoffs, then you can talk to me." Six months later, Sapp was a world champion.

• A locker room with Sapp and Keyshawn Johnson ate up its share of reporters' notepads, especially when they took on each other. "I deal with [Sapp] because I have to, not because I want to," Johnson once wrote on his website. Sapp eventually volleyed. "The thing that I'll always say is that there's never been the real deal. I want to see the wideout who's supposed to strike fear in a defense. Show me that guy." Sapp fumed over Johnson's refusal to take part in off-season workouts, especially when Gruden came on and revamped the entire offense. "We've changed quarterbacks, we've changed coordinators, we've changed systems, we've changed almost everything—everything but the way our receiver comes to work." Johnson shrugged it off, telling *The St. Petersburg Times*, "If you walk by a dog and he barks at you every day, sooner or later you just figure he'll stop barking." He didn't.

• In 2003, Sapp was warned to stop his pregame routine of running through an opponent's warm-up line. Sapp, due to make $6.6 million that year, didn't like being told what to do, blasting the NFL as "a slave system." Specifically, "Make no mistake about it, slave master say you can't do it, don't do it. They'll make an example out of you … I guess I've become larger than life." That very same week, Sapp bumped an official while running onto the field at Washington. It cost him a $50,000 fine. Larger than life? Absolutely.

Quiet Exit

As long as the Bucs were winning and Sapp was producing, his act was going to be tolerated. In 2003, neither was the case. The Bucs would spin off to their first losing season since Sapp's second year. And Sapp's play declined. Though far from ineffective, his ability to disrupt plays inside flashed far more infrequently. By midseason, he had boycotted most of Tampa's media.

When his six-year, $36 million contract expired, the Bucs did not offer Sapp an extension, allowing him to wade into the free-agent waters. More than two weeks into the process, Sapp received his first offer, from Cincinnati, but it was trumped by the one team Sapp seemed destined for all along: the Raiders.

"The big, bad silver and black and Warren Sapp coming together," he said at the introductory news conference in Oakland. "It's got to be a match made in heaven."

As for his time in Tampa Bay?

"We turned a third-world country into the Taj Mahal," Sapp said.

Derrick Brooks—Heart, Soul and Substance

A Leader of Men

Second-year offensive tackle Kenyatta Walker, a starter his entire rookie season, struggled through his second preseason and was deactivated for the 2002 opener. For Walker and his fragile psyche, it was a humiliating development that set off a profanity-laced tirade as he left the stadium following the team's loss against New Orleans in Coach Jon Gruden's first game.

The next day, Walker was summoned for a meeting with Gruden and line coach Bill Muir. Before he went in, Walker was approached by a teammate.

"Be a man in there," Brooks said.

Walker took the advice from an expert on the subject and emerged from his meeting a starter again. He also emerged a better player, better person and better teammate.

"I know what he did for me," Walker said. "I can't imagine what the team would do without him."

Modest Roots

Dungy once said of Brooks, "If I had the first pick in a pick-up game, and could choose any player in the league, he'd be my guy."

Any football person in their right mind would say the same thing.

With seven straight Pro Bowls and the 2002 NFL Defensive Player of the Year on his resume, Brooks will be in the Hall of Fame one day. But his legacy as both a person and a player was cemented long ago.

"Two things my parents always taught me: You toot your own horn you make one sound and it doesn't last long because you run out of breath. If a lot of other people are tooting your

Linebacker Derrick Brooks, an outstanding person and fan favorite, slaps hands with Bucs fans during the team's Super Bowl victory parade. (AP/WWP)

horn, it makes a lot of noise, and the sound is going to be forever because everyone is doing it," Brooks said. "Secondly, I'm not about to gain the whole world and lose my soul. That's not who I am. I'm not a loudmouth who likes to go out and talk about this or talk about that."

Had Brooks been the kind to primp, flex and play to the cameras, the Florida State product may have rivaled Ray Lewis on the publicity front. Brooks preferred the role of quiet chief. That's why a big Brooks hit is accompanied by a few subtle words whispered into the ear of the recipient.

"You've got to be humble, but you still have to have a certain swagger," Brooks said. "I'll whisper something to the guy—that's the swagger. Nobody else has to know it but me and him."

A Trophy Case Player and Man

His Sunday exploits were well documented. So were his achievements every other day of the week.

In 2000, Brooks was honored as the co-recipient of the Walter Payton/NFL Man of the Year award, the league's highest honor away from the game. In 2003, it was the Bart Starr Award, presented by Athletes In Action to the player exemplifying outstanding character and leadership in the home, on the field and in the community.

"When I receive these awards, I say it's not me, but a reflection of God's work through me," said Brooks, who got a graduate degree from FSU and was named to the school's Board of Trustees. "It's the opportunity he afforded a 160-pound linebacker from Pensacola, Florida. It's the home of Roy Jones Jr. and Emmitt Smith. I'm just a guy that God has chosen to do great work. It's His work. I'm a small part, the instrument that He's driving."

Brooks formed a group called the "Brooks Bunch," an educational/life skills program for 20 underprivileged youths in the Tampa area. In 1998, he began taking the group to places like New York, Washington, D.C., the Grand Canyon and even Africa, as well as on college tours.

"This gives me a chance to give something back," Brooks said.

During the journey to Africa, the "Bunch" took a safari-like drive into the plains. An *Animal Planet* addict, Brooks was fascinated by the big cats; the way they stalked and took down their prey. He was entranced at the sight of the cheetah.

"Not the biggest of all cats," Brooks said, "but the fastest, the most nimble, the most athletic."

A feline Brooks.

Not long after Gruden was hired, the new coach summoned his fast cat for their first face-to-face meeting.

"He sort of just stared at me for like 30 seconds before he said anything," Brooks recalled. "I was like, 'What's up with this dude?' I was like, 'Welcome, Coach, glad you're here,' but he just kept staring. Then he said, 'I'm going to need you. I'm going to need you to lead this team.' That I was a key to the transition because of what Coach Dungy had meant to everyone in that locker room and the loyalty that he'd left behind, he was asking for me to step up and help."

Gruden went to the right person.

Chapter 12

FACES OF THE FRANCHISE

Ricky Bell—Carrying a Burden

"Ricky Bell was 220 pounds of pure man."
—Linebacker David Lewis

Coach John McKay called it an easy decision. It became his most controversial one.

In 1977, the winless Bucs used the draft's first pick for USC running back Ricky Bell, a six-foot-two, 220-pound work-horse, bypassing Heisman winner Tony Dorsett of Pittsburgh.

"Ricky Bell is bigger and stronger," said McKay, who had nine former USC players (including his son) on his first roster. "We know him personally and besides, Ricky Bell is the better player."

As a rookie, Bell rushed for 436 yards (and a 2.9-yard average) and one touchdown. He played with nagging injuries—ankle, shoulder, knee, ribs—behind a porous offensive line. The constant target of wrath, Bell suffered in silence, with the notable exception of a home game against Atlanta. He tried to scale a restraining wall, in an atypical fit of rage, to get at a relentlessly razzing fan. He was pulled back by teammates and police.

Dorsett, selected second by Dallas, rushed for 1,007 yards and 12 touchdowns for the world-champion Cowboys. He was NFL rookie of the year.

"I expected to come to Tampa and rip up the league," Bell later said. "I was supposed to be the guy who led this team out of the forest. But it wasn't that easy."

Bell kept churning. By his third season, he rushed for 1,263 yards. Down the stretch, he was nearly unstoppable. In a 3-0 win against Kansas City that clinched the NFC Central Division title, Bell rushed for 137 yards on 39 carries. He added 142 yards on 38 carries (a NFL playoff record) against Philadelphia.

He was just getting started.

But the end was near.

"We didn't know he was getting sick," McKay later said.

By 1982, virtually fazed out of the offense due to fading production, a disgruntled Bell was traded to San Diego. He relished the fresh beginning, closer to his home in Los Angeles. Then one morning, he struggled to get out of bed.

Gradually, his weight dropped. Skin peeled away from his eyelids. He wore long sleeves to cover a discolored complexion. He carried only twice in 1982 before learning he had polymyositis, a rare muscular and skin disease that caused severe pain in his joints.

At the most horrifying point, Bell dropped to 110 pounds, about half his weight when he carried 51 times in a game for USC. After grudgingly retiring from the NFL, the only comeback he wanted was a healthy life. He regained most of his weight, but the complicated disease caused cardiac problems, which killed him in 1984. He was 29.

Bell left behind a widow, two children, a mother, six brothers and a legacy.

As a USC freshman, he was on academic probation. After determined offseason work, even after signing his initial million-dollar contract, he received his communications degree in '79.

"My grandchildren and great-grandchildren will want to go to college because I set the course," Bell said after graduation. The same was true in Tampa, where he set a dignified example.

Jimmie Giles—The First Weapon

"He looks like a Mack truck rolling down the freeway out there."

—Linebacker Cecil Johnson

On paper he looked like a throwaway addition to the deal. The Bucs shipped the first choice in the 1978 draft to the Houston Oilers for first- and second-rounders that year, as well as third- and fifth-rounders in 1979.

And tight end Jimmie Giles.

The Bucs used their pick to select Doug Williams. The rest of the acquisitions evaporated in Tampa Bay lore. But Giles, a little-used backup in Houston, became a star at the evolving position of tight end.

Worth noting: Giles went to Pro Bowls—four of them—during an era when Kellen Winslow and Ozzie Newsome, future Hall of Famers at the position, were there also.

Giles, who caught the winning touchdown in Tampa Bay's first postseason win, had size and speed rarely seen at the position. He caught passes in the seams and out-raced defenders to the end zone; or ran them over trying to get there.

In 1981, Giles averaged 17.5 yards per catch on 45 receptions. One of those was an 81-yard touchdown against Atlanta, a team record in length. Giles flattened a cornerback and outran a safety en route to the score, with McKay expressing his amazement afterward.

"I thought he was going to run through the end zone and all the way to Malio's for a steak," McKay said. "I don't know how he stopped."

He rarely did.

Giles was asked to define the prototype tight end.

"The prototype?" he asked. "That's for people who write stories. But I guess he is a guy who does everything for his team: run, block downfield. It depends on what a team calls a prototype. I certainly consider myself one of the best, if not the best, at what I do."

So did everybody else.

James Wilder—A Star in a Forgotten Era

"You wouldn't believe how much we all look up to him."

—Running Back Lars Tate

Had he been fortunate enough to play for a contender, James Wilder could have been a superstar in the Roger Craig mold. He was that good, but the Bucs were that bad.

Wilder did not say much, but expressed himself with a combination of speed, power and grace unparalleled by any back ever to wear the uniform.

"Even where I lived, growing up in Missouri, somehow I came to be a Buc fan," Wilder once said. "I saw all those losses,

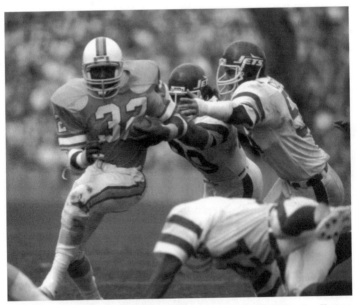

Running back James Wilder (#32) remains the franchise's all-time leading rusher. (The Tampa Tribune)

but I said to myself, 'Hey, this is a talented team. It's only a matter of time.' I was pleased and surprised to wind up in Tampa."

Drafted in the second round from Missouri in 1981, Wilder won the team's starting fullback position but didn't become the featured player in the offense until 2 1/2 seasons later. That was when McKay moved the magnificently built Wilder—six foot two and a half, 222 pounds with a 34-inch waist—to tailback and fed him the ball.

Wilder made a modest 64-yard debut in a 24-21 home loss to New Orleans. The following Sunday, he rushed for 126 yards on a league-record 42 carries, but the Bucs fell 17-12 at Pittsburgh. In the Steelers locker room, even Franco Harris was impressed.

"Forty-two carries?" asked Harris, who knew something about being a workhorse.

The next week, the 0-9 Bucs went to Minnesota. Wilder gained a franchise-record 219 yards, a mark that still stands. Tampa Bay won 17-12.

"He's the ultimate weapon," McKay said. "Unfortunately, he's also our only weapon."

In 1984, Wilder was one of the best in the game. His 407 carries were a single-season NFL record; his 1,544 yards rushing, 13 touchdowns and 85 receptions were team records.

After gaining 177 yards against the playoff-bound Giants at the Meadowlands, linebacker Lawrence Taylor called Wilder the best back he'd ever played against. Added Coach Bill Parcells: "I was impressed. I'd never seen him before in person, and I'm not sure I care to see to see him again."

Like all go-to guys, Wilder eventually broke down. By the time Ray Perkins arrived to coach the team, the carries had taken their toll. He was moved back to fullback and took on the part of a role player; he even agreed to play special teams.

The 1989 season was Wilder's last with the Bucs, as he exited the team as part of Plan-B free agency. Fifteen years later, he remains Tampa Bay's all-time record-holder in rushing yards (5,957) and receptions (430).

"When you say, 'Tampa Bay,' you should say 'James Wilder' in the same sentence," linebacker Ervin Randle said when Wilder departed. "He never got a lot of credit over the years, but he's always been the same happy guy, willing to give it all. You've got to respect a guy like that."

Everyone did.

Paul Gruber—A Pillar Cruelly Crumbles

"I wish he could be running off at Raymond James Stadium with an ovation of 70,000 people, giving him a warrior's send-off. That's what he is. A warrior."

—Offensive Guard Ian Beckles

Brenda Gruber knew something was wrong when her husband stayed down, holding his leg. Since they'd met during high school in Prairie du Sac, Wisconsin, Paul Gruber never stayed down. Ever.

She screamed for him to get up. Begged him to get up.

Then she cried.

The date was January 2, 2000, and Gruber, who extended his team record for games played to 183 that day, was welcomed to the new millennium by being carted off Soldier Field in Chicago with a broken leg. The Bucs beat the Bears 20-6, won their first NFC Central Division in 18 years and earned a bye in the playoffs.

But Gruber wouldn't play.

In fact, he'd never play again.

Even for the Bucs, this one was too twisted to be believed.

"That's life," Gruber, 35, said at the news conference announcing his retirement nine months after the injury. "You take it how you get it."

Perkins didn't do much as Tampa Bay's coach, but credit the man for selecting Gruber, one of the organization's classiest and most consistent players ever.

Armed with the fourth overall pick in the 1988 draft, Perkins gave the Bucs a pillar of power at the crucial left tackle position.

Unassuming and unexciting, Gruber played at a remarkably high level for 13 seasons. Despite a protracted holdout his rookie training camp, he was in the starting lineup at his very first NFL practice and was on the field for 4,850 consecutive plays.

Gruber never went to the Pro Bowl. Nine straight losing seasons can mask a great player. Eventually, however, Gruber's talent and professionalism were rewarded with the team's first playoff berth in 15 years. He was there—"the bedrock" of the offense, according to Warren Sapp—when the Bucs finally returned to the postseason in 1997. Gruber wasn't there when they went back in 1999 when they lost at St. Louis 11-6 in the NFC title game. A sturdy left tackle might have been the difference in a five-point game.

Either way, Gruber made a difference from the moment he arrived.

"You're talking about a guy who had virtually no training camp whatsoever. He's been learning on the run," Perkins said during Gruber's rookie season. "He started the first game, played every play, then played every play since then. He'll probably play every play for the next 12 years."

Perkins was close. Gruber missed only four games due to injury in nearly 13 years. He was a rose among the weeds in an era of bad Bucs football.

He deserved a better ending, but didn't ask for one.

"I consider myself lucky," Gruber said at his farewell. "During some of the bad times, I wanted out of here really bad. I'm so glad I stayed. This is home."

Hardy Nickerson—The Chosen One

"I think we all looked at Hardy and wondered, 'What's the deal with this guy?' It wasn't long before we knew."
—Safety John Lynch

The year was 1993. Hardy Nickerson was in the first day of training camp as a Buc, having jumped from Pittsburgh as a free agent. His teammates sensed that the excitable newcomer was different. They were sure of it when Nickerson heated up a sweltering July day by getting in the face of defensive end Keith McCants.

The fourth pick in the draft only three years earlier, McCants was a notorious underachiever. The Bucs had drafted him as a linebacker, then moved him to end, trying anything to get some productivity. Nothing worked.

Now came Nickerson.

It began with words, was followed by glares, then morphed into punches.

Stunned players watched. Coaches smiled.

McCants was later cut. Nickerson stuck around a long time. So did his attitude.

"People thought I was crazy," Nickerson said, "but I came here to win a championship."

By the time the Lombardi Trophy was raised—sometimes, no one is safe from the salary cap—Nickerson had been gone three seasons. His passion and will, however, never left the locker room.

"We were young, so we watched him," Derrick Brooks said. "We learned from him. He set the tone."

When the Bucs signed Nickerson to a three-year, $5.1 million deal in 1993, it represented one of the richest contracts in franchise history. They lured Nickerson to a bottom-feeding organization by selling the need for a passionate, respected and feared presence; a bad cop. Leave diplomacy in Pittsburgh, they added. Nickerson was promised total backing from the front office and coaching staff.

In other words, the reconstruction of the franchise—both how it played and how it was perceived—was to begin with him.

After the dustup with McCants came a brutal brawl with Tyji Armstrong, a tight end of insignificance but the most intimidating man on the team. Nickerson ripped the facemask from Armstrong's helmet and wailed away. Blood from both men was everywhere. It spilled for the next seven seasons.

Nickerson finished 1993 with a team-record 214 tackles, shattering the previous mark of 174. His vicious hits—some after the whistle—and demonstrative poses began showing up weekly on ESPN. He fed off the perception that the Bucs were starting to foster a reputation as an up-and-coming defense.

Wide receiver Lamar Thomas was Nickerson's roommate. The two waged many wars on video games.

"Hardy wants to hit hard, even on a computer," Thomas said. "There's a little ambulance that comes on the field if you really kill somebody. That's what Hardy wanted. Every time. He'd get mad. He'd say he hit the guy hard enough, so where's the ambulance?"

Nickerson was the Bucs' ambulance. He came on the field and rescued them from a mindset of sub-mediocrity. His final season with the team came in 1999. He left as the No. 1 tackler in team history. It would have been fitting had Nickerson been there when that Super Bowl title finally was won.

In so many ways, he was.

Mike Alstott—"The A-Train"

"He runs over people with that big 'ol head of his and plays offense the way us defensive guys would play over there."

—Linebacker Nate Webster

When he first entered the league, people wondered if fullback Mike Alstott represented a next-generation kind of offensive threat. At 6-1, 248 pounds, the rookie from Purdue was built

The A-Train, fullback Mike Alstott, breaks yet another tackle. (AP/WWP)

like a soda machine and, in limited duty that first season, ran defenders over at times like a vending machine on wheels.

Generation next? No. But by the time he became a regular in his second season, the "A-Train" had the adoration of next-generation Bucs fans.

"John Riggins was my sports hero," Alstott said. "He's the guy I always wanted to emulate."

Alstott never achieved the status of Riggins, a Hall of Famer. Alstott, in fact, never could wrest the job as featured runner in Tampa Bay's endless search to find an identity on offense.

"If Mike were playing in Pittsburgh or some place like that, he'd put up some pretty big numbers," Coach Tony Dungy said. "He'd probably be averaging 100 yards a game and thousand-yard seasons."

Instead, Alstott shared the workload with guys like Errict Rhett, Warrick Dunn and Michael Pittman.

He shared the adoration of the fans with no one. The sight of No. 40 jerseys at Raymond James Stadium—far and away the top-sellers in the Bay area—was proof.

Relatively quiet and ruggedly handsome, Alstott's blue-collar persona went over big in Tampa, especially with the beer-swilling working class.

"I work hard," said Alstott, the club's all-time leader in rushing touchdowns with 47 and No. 2 all-time rusher with 4,607 yards. "I've had a lot of criticism. You can't do this, you can't do that—but I still do it. I love working hard, being out there and trying to make things happen. I'm not a rah-rah guy, just someone who tries to inspire through my play."

His no-nonsense running inspired teammates, but especially the home crowd. Fans ate up his helmet-splitting style. Alstott would shed four, sometimes five defenders during a play, which made for some of the greatest single-play highlights in team history.

"Yeah, but I'd like to think over the years that I've made a move or two," Alstott said.

Any flashes of Alstott shiftiness in the open field probably had more to do with defenders' shifty (and cold) feet.

"Guys are cringing with fear that they might get run over, if you will, when they approach Mike in the open field. Accordingly, they're frozen and lock up," general manager Rich

McKay said. "Where Mike makes people miss is later in the game, when he's punished a few people along the way. And don't think they don't see that in the huddle, on the sideline or on the tape the week before."

Though most remember the Bucs' blowout of the Raiders in the Super Bowl for a defense that returned three interceptions for scores, the team's first touchdown of the day was vintage Alstott: a two-yard dive up the middle that nearly decapitated Oakland linebacker Eric Barton at the point of attack.

The image of defenders bouncing off Alstott was missed during the confounding 2003 season after Alstott suffered a neck injury against Carolina.

Though he tried to play, Alstott was placed on injured reserve a month later. His season ended with just 27 carries, a tearful news conference alongside his wife and questions about whether one of the toughest Bucs would suit up again.

The questions, of course, came from everybody but Alstott, who was cleared to return for 2004.

"Yeah, it's scary, but I guess I'm just a stubborn athlete," a healthy Alstott said after his first offseason practice. "I was coming back ... and there was never a doubt in my mind."

Warrick Dunn—Diminutive Man, Gigantic Heart

"We never viewed drafting him as a risk. He always made big plays in big games, and he could always change the game with one play."
—Director of College Personnel Tim Ruskell

Warrick Dunn was either sized up or downsized.

Third-down specialist.

Scatback.

Not durable enough.

"The stereotypes have always been there," Dunn said.

But the Bucs had a solid perception of Dunn, who stood five foot eight on his tiptoes and was charitably listed at 180 pounds. He made defenders miss and never took a clean shot. The Bucs saw someone who could change a game simply by squeezing through a sliver of an opening.

Shortly after drafting Dunn from FSU as a first-rounder in 1997, the Bucs learned they'd also added a player who wanted to change people's lives.

When Dunn was a high school senior in Baton Rouge, Louisana, his mother, a police corporal, was murdered. Through the trauma, he dealt with reality. He was left with five younger siblings to whom he became father and protector.

"There are tough situations families have to deal with," Dunn said. "Sometimes, we all could use a little help from somebody."

That was the motivation for Dunn's "Homes For The Holidays" program. He paid the down payments on homes for low-income families with single mothers, a cause close to his heart. He made a few dreams come true.

Dunn's sleepy eyes and wisp-like presence were deceptive. He stood tall. It was a quality the Bucs noticed at the annual NFL Combine in Indianapolis. Beyond the meat-market backdrop, where coaches and scouts measure, weigh and compare the athletic products on display, there are the private conversations, the job interviews.

"Warrick Dunn was the most impressive person we ever spoke with in that setting," McKay said.

There was sincerity and an earnest desire to succeed. Some teams were concerned about Dunn's size and ability to perform as a feature back. But weren't the same things once said about Barry Sanders? The Bucs were sold.

As a rookie, Dunn was a slippery and elusive counter to the pile-driving Alstott, giving Tampa Bay an ideal mix of speed and power. But Dunn's greatest contributions were reserved for the 2000 season, when Alstott went down with a knee injury. Dunn rushed for 767 yards and seven touchdowns in the final eight games, including a 210-yard outburst against Dallas that ranks second only to Wilder's single-game mark.

And along the way, maybe he shattered a few stereotypes.

"If I touch the ball, the possibilities are there," said Dunn, who left for Atlanta via free agency in 2002 with 4,200 career rushing yards. Too small?

"Most guys take direct hits," he said. "I don't."

Ronde Barber—The Twin

"You can't measure instinct and desire."
—Secondary Coach Mike Tomlin

Within three hours, identical twins Tiki and Ronde Barber were drafted by NFL teams in 1997. Both had been academic and athletic superstars—side by side—at Cave Spring High in Roanoke, Virginia, and later at the University of Virginia, where Tiki left as the school's career rushing leader and Ronde started every game for three years at cornerback.

In a crowded restaurant celebrating their draft-day moment, mother Geraldine Barber cried as Ronde got off his cell phone with Dungy, whose team had taken Barber in the third round. Tiki had gone in the second to the Giants.

After shaking hands and embracing bodies, Ronde and Tiki excused themselves from the party and walked off to a corner to share a moment alone.

After 22 inseparable years, it was time.

"Basically, it was our first goodbye," Ronde said. "We were a ways away from actually packing up, getting in the cars and driving off, but our ride, if you will, was done and the two of us realized it. The rec league success, the high school success and college success had led us to that very moment ... and now it was over. We'd spent our lives pretty much doing the same things. Now, we were going to be on our own."

Not exactly. Even 1,200 miles apart, the Barbers never left each other's side. They stayed in constant communication, sometimes five or six calls a day, as their careers soared a parallel plane to stardom.

Tiki was the first to break out. His 1999 season in the Big Apple put him on the map, but it was Ronde who played in the NFC Championship Game that year.

In 2000, Tiki and the Giants made it to Super Bowl XXXV; in Tampa, no less. Ronde was ecstatic for this brother and smiled sibling pride while the two hung out that week. Unfortunately, the Ravens hung a 34-7 beating on the Giants.

Two years later, it was Tiki's turn to watch and cheer.

And celebrate.

The fame gained from their popular Visa commercials and co-selection as one of *People Magazine's* 50 Most Beautiful People paled in comparison to seeing through a world title.

Barber's 92-yard interception return to seal the NFC Championship Game affirmed the Bucs' champion attitude. They had been talking big for years and had it thrown back in their faces when the quest fell short.

But Barber played a great corner that day; and a better closer.

"I'm not scared to admit it—we're good, really good," Barber beamed afterward.

While Lynch was the captain of the defense and leader of the secondary, Barber grew into the playmaker. He developed into a cornerstone, tying the team record with league-high 10 interceptions that got him to the Pro Bowl following the 2001 season. The Bucs' vaunted "cover two" defensive scheme was built around Brooks, but it couldn't work without a ball-hawking, sure-tackling cornerback manning the underneath zone.

"Did you guys see Ronde Barber out there today?" defensive coordinator Monte Kiffin asked. "Man!"

Barber just might have played the perfect game against the Eagles: six tackles, four passes defended, a sack, a forced fumble and a maybe the signature play in Tampa Bay history.

"For me, this is hard to put in perspective," said Barber, overwhelmed by the moment yet cognizant of a task still at hand. "But we've got something bigger yet to accomplish. We're on a path of destiny and we don't want to mess it up now."

A week later, Tiki watched the Super Bowl at his brother's side; more specifically, on the Tampa Bay sideline, where they shared another hug neither will forget.

Celebrate the Heroes of Professional Football
in These Other 2004 Releases from Sports Publishing!

Marv Levy: Where Else Would You Rather Be?
by Marv Levy

- 6 x 9 hardcover
- 250 pages
- photos throughout
- $24.95

Riddell Presents: The Gridiron's Greatest Quarterbacks
by Jonathan Rand

- 9 x 12 hardcover
- 140 pages
- color photos throughout
- $24.95

Roger Craig's Tales from the San Francisco 49ers Sideline
by Roger Craig with Matt Maiocco

- 5.5 x 8.25 hardcover
- 200 pages
- photos throughout
- $19.95

Sam Wyche's Tales from the Cincinnati Bengals Sideline
by Sam Wyche with Matt Fulks

- 5.5 x 8.25 hardcover
- 200 pages
- photos throughout
- $19.95

Game of My Life: 25 Stories of Packers Football
by Chuck Carlson

- 6 x 9 hardcover
- 250 pages
- photos throughout
- $24.95

Legends of the Dallas Cowboys
by Cody Monk

- 8.5 x 11 hardcover
- 180 pages
- color photos throughout
- $24.95

The Golden Voices of Football
by Ted Patterson

- 10.25 x 10.25 hardcover
- photos/illustrations throughout
- 200 pages • $29.95
- Includes an audio CD!

Steve McMichael's Tales from the Bears Sideline
by Steve McMichael with Phil Arvia

- 5.5 x 8.25 hardcover
- 200 pages
- photos throughout
- $19.95

Steve Raible's Tales from the Seahawks Sideline
by Steve Raible with Mike Sando

- 5.5 x 8.25 hardcover
- 200 pages
- photos throughout
- $19.95

Dante Hall: X-Factor
by Dante Hall with Bill Althaus

- 8.5 x 11 hardcover
- 128 pages
- color photos throughout
- $24.95

To order at any time, please call toll-free **877-424-BOOK (2665)**.
For fast service and quick delivery, order on-line at **www.SportsPublishingLLC.com**.